MW00573190

How to Build a

PROFITABLE

Nonprofit Organization:

A Step by Step Guide to A Fully Funded Nonprofit Organization

Crystal R. Durham

Copyright

How to Build a Profitable Nonprofit Organization: A Step by Step Guide to A Fully Funded Nonprofit Organization © 2020

Crystal R. Durham

Printed in the United States of America

ISBN: 978-1-7349750-0-0

All rights reserved. No part of this book may be reproduced in any form or by any electronic, mechanical or photocopying or stored in a retrieval system without the written permission of the publisher except by a reviewer who may quote brief passages to be included in a review.

Scriptures marked KJV are taken from the KING JAMES VERSION (KJV): KING JAMES VERSION, public domain.

Scripture quotations marked (NIV) are taken from the Holy Bible, New International Version®, NIV®. Copyright © 1973, 1978, 1984, 2011 by Biblica, Inc.® Used by permission of Zondervan. All rights reserved worldwide. www.zondervan.com The "NIV" and "New International Version" are trademarks registered in the United States Patent and Trademark Office by Biblica, Inc.®

Scriptures marked TM are taken from the THE MESSAGE: THE BIBLE IN CONTEMPORARY ENGLISH (TM): Scripture taken from THE MESSAGE: THE BIBLE IN CONTEMPORARY ENGLISH, copyright©1993, 1994, 1995, 1996, 2000, 2001, 2002. Used by permission of NavPress Publishing Group

The American Standard Version (ASV) of the Holy Bible was first published in 1901 by Thomas Nelson & Sons. This translation of the Holy Bible is in the public domain, since its copyright has expired and is the predecessor to the New American Standard Bible.

TABLE OF CONTENTS

INTRODUCTION

R ight now, in this very moment, I am not sure if it was ever "in" me to write a book. Whenever I ponder the thought, my mind instantly floods with uncertainties. What would I write about? Who would be interested in reading, my thoughts or life story? Am I qualified to teach others? Even as I sit here writing the first chapter of this book, I ask myself "What qualifies me to teach you how to build a profitable nonprofit? Well, after a long review of my life at 58 years young, an honest conversation with God, and support from my husband – I discovered the answer to that question. And here it is. Back in 1972, I was kicked out of high school and banned from attending any other school in my hometown of Wilmington, Delaware. So without a diploma or GED, at the age of 20, I found myself pregnant with my oldest child my son, Kasyi. And instead of planning a gender reveal celebration like the millennials of today, I was weighed down by the words of one of my high school teachers. His voice repeated over and over in my head, "You will never be anything but a whore having a bunch of babies, living off of food stamps in the projects.

I needed to prove him wrong. While pregnant, I struggled, but I earned my GED, and worked full-time to provide for my child. The struggle was real, and it made me stronger. Not only did I prove him wrong, but I proved to myself that I was resilient.

By the age of twenty-five, I was the mother of two beautiful children, and I was not living in the projects nor was I living off of welfare. Over the years, I have guided countless youth from helpless to hopeful mindsets through sheer and unconditional love.

I am a wife, the mother of ten children in a blended family. In 2018, my husband and I adopted four of my sister's children.

As a little girl, I too, experienced the pain of many youth today. By the age of 28, I had been kidnapped, molested, raped, verbally/physically abused, homeless and diagnosed an alcoholic. Through these firsthand experiences, I have learned that if God brought me out of one bad situation after the next, God can do the same for every youth who wants it.

Today, I am....I am a successful serial-entrepreneur as CEO of Ninety Days of Love Crisis Center, Inc. for Aged out Foster Care Youth, CEO of Crystal R. Durham, a non-profit professional coach, and CEO of 90 Day Housing for re-entry women. In addition, I'm the Co-CEO of 50/50 Mentoring for girls 12 to 18 years old. God has equipped and qualified me to empower them to believe, achieve, and dream beyond limitation. My strong desire is for every young person to know God's **True Love** *"He Knows."*

My Synopsis

I think back to a time before I launched Ninety Days of Love Crisis Center. I was at work one day, and I remember feeling completely empty inside. It was a feeling I had never felt before, and for some strange reason I began to ask myself a few questions. If I died today or tomorrow, what would people say about me? Whose life did I personally impact? What legacy will I leave behind? My eyes began to fill with tears, and my heart slowly filled with sadness. I turned to my supervisor at the time and said, "I want to impact the lives of young people." And to my surprise she said,

"Then go ahead and do it." A month later, I launched my nonprofit organization, and I was fired from my job. This pushed me into my destiny, and I went in with both feet running. I registered for school to gain knowledge on the best practices of running a successful 501©3 nonprofit organization. On the very first day of class, my coach read scriptures and addressed our nonprofit organization as our ministry. She read *Psalms 127:1 "Unless the Lord builds the house, they labor in vain who build it."*

When I started my nonprofit, I had no idea I was going to be doing ministry. I often joked with God, saying He tricked me because if I knew this was ministry, I probably would have run 100mph in the opposite direction. If you are reading this book, it is because HE has called you to do ministry for a reason, and it's not just because you have gone through some things. He has called you to start your nonprofit (ministry) organization because He can trust you to get the job done. With that being said, let's get started.

Like many of you, I had no clue what I needed to do or how I was going to get it done. I Googled and Googled for weeks until I found something like this.

DEDICATION

I dedicate this book to my mother, Dorothy J. Taylor. She is the reason I can freely share my life story. I remember calling her and asking her for her permission to share my experiences. In her soft voice, she asked, "Will it help somebody?" I said, "Yes," then she replied, "Share your story!" I love you mom, and thanks for believing in me.

I also dedicate this book to my daughter, Cheri M. Felton. I'm so proud of the woman you have become. I thank God for you and for your obedience and non-judgmental spirit. I love you so much.

Finally, I dedicate this book to my husband, Michael N. Durham. You are the man I needed in my life for such a time as this. I thank God for you allow me to be all that God has called me to be. My life would not have been the same without you. I truly found the love I needed in you. Thank You.

Dear Nonprofit Professionals:

It is my great pleasure to address you for the first time in my first self-help business book on *How to Build a Profitable Non-Profit*. As the founder of Ninety Days of Love Crisis Center, Inc., an educator, entrepreneur, and nonprofit professionals' coach, I am passionate about helping other nonprofit professionals build impactful, profitable nonprofits (ministry). Since the start of my own nonprofit (ministry) in 2015, I have been able to secure **OVER 85K** from corporate sponsors, partners, and donors. I'm proof that even small nonprofits (ministry) can make **BIG** impacts in the community. And now, I'm thrilled to share my blueprint with other individuals looking to start, build, or grow their nonprofits (ministry).

I'm looking forward to helping you build upon the incredible work that you have already done to empower others. I know that with my knowledge, experience, and proven strategies we can change the national dialogue of what startup nonprofits (ministries) are able to accomplish. The families in our communities are our issues, as well as our nation's issues. We must focus on equipping our communities with the tools to overcome issues of economy, education, sexual health, mental health, employment, financial literacy, law issues, and homelessness.

Thank you for making a difference,

Crystal R. Durham, Nonprofit Professional Coach

www.crystalrdurham.com

crystalrdurham@gmail.com

404-484-3901

In life, we sometimes put the cart before the horse. You are probably thinking, "What does that have to do with starting my nonprofit ministry?" According to hindermangroup.com, there are about 314 million people in the US right now. A recent LIMRA study says that 52 million people, who make between $50,000 and $250,000 in annual income, don't have any life insurance. This means that 1,139 people in that income range die every day without life insurance. Have you ever heard of a succession plan? Well, neither did I until I started my nonprofit ministry organization. Let me explain it this way; a succession plan is like having life insurance or a will.

Have a Plan of Action - Listening Prayer

Titus 1:5 (NIV) 5 "The reason I left you in Crete was that you might put in order what was left unfinished and appoint elders in every town, as I directed you."

CHAPTER 1
SECURE THE NONPROFIT MINISTRY

Why Do I Need a Succession Plan for a Nonprofit?

According to several websites such as boardsource.org, successperformancesolutions.com, and forbes.com, there is an abundance of information to help guide you on how, what, and why it's important to secure a succession plan for your nonprofit ministry organization.

A succession plan helps businesses identify the key roles in their companies and the employee's best suited to fill those roles in the future. It establishes a trajectory for each role, highlighting the skills needed for optimal performance in each role and how those skills can be acquired.

What is the First Step in Succession Planning?

The first step in succession planning is to identify the current or future key positions or groups in the organization. At this stage, identifying key positions thoughtfully should be your only focus rather than candidates.

What is the Objective of Succession Planning?

Succession planning aims to attract the best talent, retain those individuals, and develop them through well-targeted development efforts. Succession planning helps build the bench strength of an organization to ensure the long-term health, growth and stability.

How to Develop a Succession Plan

1. Determine the type of plan.

2. Put a succession-planning team together.

3. Identify the main factors that will influence your plan.

4. Link your succession plan to your organization's overall strategic plan.

5. Identify sources for successor candidates.

6. Shape action plans.

7. Be proactive with succession planning.

8. Keep an open mind.

9. Make the vision known.

10. Offer regular feedback to protégés.

11. Provide training to peak performers.

When Should a Succession Plan be used?

This means that every organization - regardless of size - should start succession planning as early as possible because grooming leaders for high-level roles isn't something that can be achieved overnight. It can take a long, long time before they are ready to make the switch with a more senior staff member.

How Long Does it Take to Complete a Succession Plan?

As a practical matter, it typically takes two to six months to complete a succession. Some successions remain open for years due to complexity, litigation between the heirs, or a number of other reasons.

Why Do Succession Plans Fail?

Documenting a succession plan is only the first step on a journey. One reason that so many successions fail so quickly is that new hires often do not fit into the organization's culture (or powerful subcultures) well enough to do what is needed in ways that will be accepted by the people they have been hired to lead.

Succession Plan Document Example

COUNTY OF DEKALB STATE OF GEORGIA

I, _____, (hereinafter principal), a resident of DeKalb County, Georgia, do hereby continue and appoint _____ AND BOARD OF DIRECTORS for me and give such person the power(s) specified below to act in name of CEO, Organization name, and stead in any way which I myself, could do if I were personally present with respect to the following matters:

(1). Business access and all monetary transactions: to make, receive, sign, endorse, execute, acknowledge, deliver, and possess checks, drafts, bills of exchange, letters of credit, notes, donation, stock certificates, withdrawal receipts and deposit instruments relating to accounts or deposits in, or certificates of deposit of banks, savings and loans, credit union, or other institutions or associations.

(2). Business Property Transactions: to lease, sell, mortgage, purchase, exchange, and acquire, and to agree, bargain, and contract for the lease, sale purchase, exchange, and acquisition of, and to accept, take, receive, and possess any personal property whatsoever, tangible or intangible, or interest thereto, on such terms and conditions, and under such covenants, as my Agent shall deem proper; and to maintain, repair, improve, manage, insure, rent, lease, sell, convey, subject to liens or mortgages, or to take any other security interests is said property which are recognized under the Uniform Commercial Code as adopted at that time under all or any part of any real or personal property whatsoever, tangible or intangible, or any interest therein, such covenants, as my Agent shall deem proper.

(3). Safe Deposits: To have free access at any time or times to any safe deposit or vault to which (name of organization)_____ has access.

(4). Business Operating Transactions: To conduct, engage in, and otherwise transact the affairs of any and all lawful business ventures of whatever nature or kind that I may now or hereafter be involved in.

(5). Chair Board Name and Board of Directors will conduct regular monthly meetings with the staff/volunteers to make sure all business is being conducted as such. Name of CEO, Name of Organization,_____ is a non-profit organization and will continue to act as such.

On this day_____ I,_____in sound mind authorize all the above.

On this day_____ I, _____in sound mind agree to all the above.

Completing a Succession Plan is one of the most important documents to sitting your nonprofit ministry up for success. I put this first and foremost, because many nonprofit ministries do not know the importance of having such a plan in place. As you are growing your nonprofit ministry, with keeping this in mind, you and your board will be able to vote on who and what is best for the nonprofit ministry organization.

Who is Waiting on You? - Listening Prayer

Acts 3:1-8 (MSG)

Here is an illustration of God using ministry representatives to restore His people.

"One day at three o'clock in the afternoon, Peter and John were on their way into the Temple for prayer meeting. At the same time there was a man crippled from birth being carried up. Every day he sat down at the Temple gate, the one named Beautiful, to beg from those going into the Temple. When he saw Peter and John about to enter the Temple, he asked for a handout. Peter, with John at his side, looked him straight in the eye and said, 'Look here.' He looked up, expecting to get something from them. Peter said, 'I don't have a nickel to my name, but what I do have, I give you: In the name of Jesus Christ of Nazareth, walk!' He grabbed him by the right hand and pulled him up. In an instant his feet and ankles became firm. He jumped to his feet and walked."

Have you ever been a lame man; broken, desperate, and asking for the wrong thing! How many times do we do that? He was asking for alms, when what he really needed was healing. But he did not think this was possible.

He was defined by his lame condition for his entire life. Who is waiting on you? When we take the time to really seek God and ask Him for what we need, then and only then, will we be able to truly fulfill the needs of others.

CHAPTER 2
WRITE THE VISION

When you Google how to start a nonprofit, you will get something like this:

Eight Steps to Start a Nonprofit.

1. Start by developing your vision and mission. A vision is an inspiration and aspirational destination on the horizon...

2. Next you need a name...

3. Differentiate your charity...

4. Write a plan...

5. Register as a 501(c)(3)...

6. Start your website...

7. Fundraising...

8. Establish an Advisory Board...

Sounds easy right? However; it left out a few steps or twenty-two steps and most importantly it left out the step by step guide on how to accomplish each task.

Let's start with what the word says:

Habakkuk 2:2 (NIV)

"I will stand at my watch and station myself on the ramparts; I will look to see what he will say to me, and what answer I am to give to this complaint. Then the LORD replied, 'Write down the revelation and make it plain on tablets so that a herald may run with it."

Writing out the Vision

A **vision** is defined as inspiration and aspirational destination on the horizon. It should not include quantitative measures but descriptions of what you want to create. Vision Statement (What is the vision God has given you to fulfill) A vision statement is a declaration of an organization's objectives intended to guide its internal decision-making. The vision is the bigger picture and future oriented while the mission is more immediately focused on the present. Often times when God gives us a vision it is bigger than we could imagine and sometimes it may even become intimidating. Take my advice. Tell God, "This is not my vision. It is yours, and you have to show me how to bring it to pass. Now, here is an **example** of our **Vision Statement for Ninety Days of Love Crisis Center, Inc. – to assist youth in their transition to self-sufficiency.** You want to make it clear and concise for the group or community you are called to serve. Now is the time to write the vision and make it clear. Write your Vision:_____

_____

_____

Congratulations! You have written your vision and it's clear.

Now for Your Mission

The mission is a clearer and concise expression of the basic purpose of the organization:

- What is the purpose of your organization?

- Who does your organization service?

- What are the basic services of your nonprofit ministry?

Missions should be values, the beacon by which your organization will be led.

Missions Statement: (How are you going to bring the vision to past?) A formal mission statement is a summary of the aims and values of an organization mission statement to which all can subscribe. **For example: Ninety Days of Love Crisis Center, Inc. includes much more than just fulfilling a youth's basic needs – it's about building a foundation of safety and trust. Our first step is to address their immediate needs – a warm meal, a shower, the chance wear clean clothes, and to sleep in a bed.**

When setting your vision and your mission statements, try not to make it too lengthy; save that for the business plan. Write your mission_____

_____

_____

Congratulations! You have completed the most important portions of starting your nonprofit ministry. You have your vision and mission statement; therefore, you know the objectives of your nonprofit ministry and how you plan to operationalize it all.

Have you been chosen? - Listening Prayer

Matthew 22:14 (KJV)

"For many are called, but few are chosen. We know this was part of a parable of the wedding feast and many were called to be invited to the wedding but chose to make accurses."

Matthew 22:9. (KJV)

"Therefore, go into the highways and as many as you find, invite to the wedding." (Bad and good)"

There are people, both good and bad, called to be a part of your mission. When we look at the vast expanse of creation, we wonder how God could be concerned for people who constantly disappointed him. When God considered you for the mission, He already had your help and the provision for it. When we remain focused on the Great Commission, God will see our mission to the end.

CHAPTER 3
I WILL MAKE YOUR NAME GREAT!

N aming a nonprofit (ministry) seems like a simple task. Would you believe I didn't even realize I needed a name? Funny, right? Well, the only nonprofits I knew of were local churches, and huge national nonprofit (ministry) organizations. Why would little old me need to create a fancy name just to help my community? See, I told you I was lost, right?

In 2002, I actually kind of fell into my nonprofit (ministry). My daughter was about 15 or 16 years old, and she was sort of a popular student in school. However, I really never cared for popular kids because of my past experience as an adolescent. You guessed it; they were very mean to me and my friends. You would call them bullies in today's time.

Anyway, I wanted to make sure my daughter was being a good example of what a *popular* girl should be. One day, I challenged her to go to school and befriend someone who didn't look like her, smell like her, or act like her. To my surprise, she did just that! On a random day, my daughter comes home from school with the teen girl she had befriended. I called the teen's mother and went to her home for a formal meeting. The family actually lived in the same neighborhood where I was raised, around the corner from the building where I grew up. Her mother gave her and her twin sister permission to stay with us for a weekend. Now this sister, let's just say she wasn't very nice, but nonetheless allowed her to come as well.

At this time in my life, I was an entrepreneur, co-pastor of a church with my ex-husband and was raising 4 children, two of which were my baby sisters. As the twins' visits became more frequent – you can imagine my house had gotten quite busy. Their weekend visits turned into week visits. Within a few months, they moved in. Shortly after, I received a phone call from a pastor friend of mine who had a family in need of my assistance. She was a single mother with a teen daughter. The two were clashing and needed a mediator. He said he heard I was taking in troubled teens and wanted me to meet with them to see if I could possibly offer some of my services. Umm, I didn't know I offered services. Reluctantly, I said, "Yes." Then, I agreed to meet with them. I met with the family and was asked how soon the teen girl could reside in my home.

I had no plan, no program, and certainly no services. When the mother asked how long her daughter could stay in our home, I heard the Lord say "90 Days." The next month it was the same thing.

A friend called me and asked if I could please help this single mom with her

fourteen-year-old daughter. Once I heard her story, I had to meet her and see how I could help in any way possible. As she shared her story with me, it literally broke my heart into pieces. I was her story, so I understood her pain and struggles. Before I knew it, I had several young ladies living in my home for 90 days. I had no plan, no program, and no services, but what I did have was the love of God, and that's what I shared. Through sharing the love of God, those young girls' lives were changed.

Years later, I moved to Atlanta with my two sons after my divorce. I was in a class called Dream Builders to start what I thought was a daycare business. I remember it like it was yesterday. After class one day, one of my sisters in Christ walked up and stated, "I'm glad you are opening up a daycare." I smiled and then she said something I would've never imagined her saying. She said, "The daycare is a part of what you are supposed to be doing, but God has something bigger. Just as she was speaking to me, I heard the Lord say to me *Ninety Days of Love*, and all I could do was cry. That night, I stayed up for 24 hours without sleep and did my research on the community of youth He wanted me to help. I wrote out the vision, mission, and the business (ministry) plan all in one night. You see, I didn't come up with the name. He gave me the name and the mission.

Choose a name:

Genesis 12:2 (KJV) "'I'll make you a great nation and bless you. I'll make you famous; you'll be a blessing. I'll bless those who bless you;

Most nonprofits (ministry) establish their names before writing a **vision** and **mission** statement, and that's okay. Names can describe the function of the organization such as: The Red Cross, but also many successful organizations are named for people like Susan G. Komen for the Cure. A name of organizations in memory of specific people, but with a mission to help others is a great way to encourage donations. Now, let me make one thing clear. When you are naming your organization after a loved one, I don't recommend using foundation at the end of the name. **Here is why: According to investopedia.com, a private foundation is a non-profit charitable entity, which is generally created by a single benefactor, usually an individual or business. A public charity uses publicly-collected funds to directly support its initiatives. The only substantive difference between the two is the manner in which funds are acquired. (Aug 23, 2019).**

Foundations are **organizations** that do not qualify as public charities. They are very similar to nonprofits, except money for a foundation usually comes from a family or a corporate entity, whereas nonprofit money often comes from their revenues. Therefore, unless your family comes from money or your business is funding the organization, it shouldn't be a foundation.

According to the IRS, the name of your nonprofit corporation should not be the same as another corporation on file with your state's corporation's office (usually the Secretary of State's office). It should end with a corporate designator, such as

"Corporation, "Incorporated," or an abbreviation of any of those words. Your state's corporation's office can tell you how to find out whether your proposed name is available for your use. For a small fee, of $25 you can usually reserve the name for a short period of time until you file your articles of incorporations. For more information, contact your state's corporation's office.

Differentiate Your Nonprofit Ministry

The National Center of Charitable Statistics (NCCS) states there are over 1.5 million nonprofit organizations in the U.S. Many of the organizations are in competition with one another for funding to support the same cause. Therefore, you have to be clear on how your organization is different, in hope to stimulate the same kind of passion in potential donors to your organization that you have for it. Differentiating your nonprofits from all the other nonprofits can make a world of difference. Getting people to believe and donate to your nonprofit ministry will make a huge impact on your community where your organization is serving. I recommend you go to the **Secretary of State** and perform a name search. If the name is available, you can do one of two things. **1.** Pay to hold the name for 30 days. **2.** Go ahead and file your articles of incorporation while the name is available. Be sure to register your name at Secretary of State in your State. Once you file your articles of incorporation, the name is registered.

Example:

1. The Dream Team, Inc.

2. The Dream Shop, Inc.

3. The Dream Factory, Inc.

Congratulations! Now that you have a name for your nonprofit organization, and it is legally registered, let's move on.

Jesus Promises He will Take Care of us - Listening Prayer

John 14:1-7 (KJV)

"Do not let your hearts be troubled. You believe in God; believe also in me.

CHAPTER 4
OPERATING IN ORDER

O ne of my biggest rules, when starting a business (ministry), is that you must abide by the laws. Most people question if it's okay to file for their organization's EIN number before being legalized. Here are some answers to questions concerning that.

My rule of thumb is to file for INC or LLC before obtaining your EIN number. The new regulation of the IRS requires filing the articles of incorporation and other documentation before businesses can obtain an EIN.

Does a Nonprofit Need Articles of Incorporation?

According to some amazing sites such as upcounsel.com, nonprofitally.com, and harborcompliance.com, here is some information that can aid you. In order to form a nonprofit corporation, you must file articles of incorporation (sometimes called a "certificate of incorporation" or "charter document" or "articles of organization") with the state and pay a filing fee.

You must file articles of incorporation within the state's corporate filing office. In this document, you fill out some basic information such as your nonprofit's name and office address. Although preparing this document isn't difficult, you do need to include specific language to ensure that you'll receive tax-exempt status. Not only will you file articles of incorporation you will also need to generate a written copy of articles of incorporation for your board. No matter what it is, the Bible always has an answer for how we should respond to matters.

Romans 13:1 (MSG)

"Be a good citizen. All governments are under God. Insofar as there is peace and order, it's God's order. So live responsibly as a citizen."

Here is a sample of what standard written articles of incorporation language looks like; however, each state has its own language.

ARTICLES OF INCORPORATION

OF

_____

I

A. This organization is a nonprofit public benefit corporation and is not organized for the private gain of any person. It is organized under the Nonprofit Public Benefit Corporation Law for charitable purposes.

B. The specific purposes for which this corporation is organized include but are not limited to: (the preservation and management of programs educational, skills, recreational, job trainings, or open space opportunities.)

II

Name

Address

City, State zip code

III

A. The property of this corporation is irrevocably dedicated to charitable purposes, and no part of the net income or assets of the corporation shall ever inure to the benefit of any director, trustee, member or officer of this corporation, or to any private person.

B. Upon the dissolution or winding up of the corporations, any assets remaining after payment of or provision for payment of, all debts and liabilities shall be distributed to a governmental entity described in Section 170(b) (1) (A) (v) of the Internal Revenue Code, or to a nonprofit fund, foundation, or corporation which is organized and operated exclusively for charitable purposes, which has established its tax exempt status under Section 501(c)(3) of the Internal Revenue Code, and which is qualified to receive "qualified conservation contributions" within the meaning of Section 170(h) of said code, or the corresponding provisions of any future statute of the United States.

C.   In the event of a liquidation of this corporation, all corporate assets shall be disposed of in such a manner as may be directed by decree of the superior court for the county in which the corporation has its principal office, on petition therefore by the Attorney General of by any person concerned in the dissolution, in a proceeding to which the Attorney General is a party.

IN WITNESSES WHEREOF, the undersigned, being the Incorporators of_____ and the initial directors named in these Articles of Incorporation on _____, 20_____.

INCORPORATORS

Name and address_____

Vice President

Name and Address_____

Director of Board

Name and address_____

Secretary Name and address_____

Treasure Name and address _____

DECLARATION

We are the persons whose names are subscribed above. We collectively are all of the incorporators of _____.
And all of the initial directors named in the Articles of Incorporations, and we have executed these Articles of Incorporation. The foregoing Articles of Incorporation are out act and deed, joint and severally.

Executed at__,_____, we, and each of us, declare that the Foregoing is true and correct.

Congratulations! You have filed your articles of incorporation.

Are you Willing to Follow? - Listening Prayer

Luke 9:23 (NIV)

'Whoever wants to be my disciple must deny themselves and take up their cross daily and follow me."

CHAPTER 5
FOLLOWING THE LAWS OF THE LAND

Do I need Bylaws?

Several different websites have helped me answer these Bylaw questions; upcounsel.com, nonprofitally.com, and more. Here is some information that can aid you as well. A nonprofit is a form of business and is thus regulated by states. To be incorporated, an organization must have a set of bylaws. Incorporation requires you to set up all the legal requirements such as bylaws that the IRS looks for when granting tax exemption. Bylaws are the legally binding rules that outline how the board of a nonprofit will operate. While they are unique to each organization, bylaws generally have a similar structure and use.

What is the Purpose of Bylaws?

The purpose of nonprofit bylaws, and what purposes do they play? Bylaws are simply rules that help everyone to understand how the organization runs. Their role is to establish procedures for holding different elections, membership structure, quorum requirements, and many other aspects of the nonprofit.

Is Nonprofit Organizations Required to have Bylaws?

Bylaws are an organization's internal operating rules. Federal tax law does require specific language in the bylaws of most organizations. State law may require nonprofit corporations to have bylaws, and nonprofit organizations generally find it advisable to have internal operating rules.

What Should Nonprofit Bylaws Include?

Bylaws should include, at a minimum, the following:

- Governance Structure - It is important to understand whether the organization is board driven or member driven. If the corporation is board driven, there are typically no members or the members have very limited rights. This shouldn't be the case for a nonprofit organization.

Are Nonprofit Bylaws Public Record?

Bylaws are not public documents but making them readily available increases your accountability and transparency and encourage your board to pay closer attention to them. Your board should review them regularly and amend them accordingly as your organization evolves.

Are Articles of Incorporation the Same as Bylaws?

Articles of incorporation and bylaws are not the same; let's look at the difference between bylaws and articles of incorporation. Bylaws and articles of incorporation are a corporation's official documents for organizing, governing and operating. Incorporation is a legal process governed by the state. The bylaws set forth the internal operating rules that the corporation must follow and detail the roles of board members and officers. The bylaws and articles of incorporation have similarities, but the primary differences make both documents necessary for creating the corporation's legal structure.

Articles of incorporation are public records; **bylaws** are not. ... For a corporation, this document is called **articles of incorporation** and **articles of organization** for a limited liability company (LLC) according to bizfiling.com

What Happens if a Nonprofit Does Not Follow its Bylaws?

Failing to follow the articles or bylaws of the organization can lead to consequences for the organization itself and its board members. Another common issue is the Board's failure to abide by its own articles or bylaws. One of the most common pitfalls for nonprofits is often failure to file a Form 990 in a timely manner. Your Board of Directors is responsible for making sure your board members are operating in the matter of the bylaws and its articles of incorporation are vital to your organization.

What the Bible says about the Bylaws?

Joshua 1:8 (KJV)

"This book of the law shall not depart out of thy mouth; but thou shalt meditate therein day and night, that thou mayest observe to do according to all that is written therein: for then thou shalt make thy way prosperous, and then thou shalt have good success.

Here is what Cumin Written Bylaws looks like for the state of Georgia (note, they may vary from state to state).

Bylaws

For

Nonprofit Organization Form Example

Internal rules and procedures for _____
existence and responsibilities of corporate offices hold organization accountable, aid in the setting up of policy and procedures, regularly attends board meetings and important related meetings. Must commit to actively participate in committee events voluntarily and stay informed about committee matters, prepare themselves well for meetings, and review comments on minutes and reports. To keep the mission of _____ in for front of everything we do here at _____.
Get to know other committee members and build a good working relationship that contributes to consensus, be an active participant in the committee's annual evaluation and planning efforts. Directors should participate 100% in fund raising for the organization (nonprofit only) starting with board giving first. Create fundraiser for the organization and find donors for the organization. _____ Have nine active Boards of Directors and their term is one - two years, then the board votes. The Board of Directors meet every month for the first six months then every three months. Thereafter, the Chair Director may call for a meeting, and the board will vote on matters to the best interest of the organization.

Violations of the Conflicts of Interest Policy:

a. If the governing board or committee has reasonable cause to believe a director has failed to disclose actual or possible conflicts of interest, it shall inform the member of the basis for such belief and afford the member an opportunity to explain the alleged failure to disclose.

b. If, after hearing the member's response and after making further investigation as warranted by the circumstances, the governing board or committee determines the member has failed to disclose an actual or possible conflict of interest, it shall take appropriate disciplinary and corrective action.

Records of Proceedings

The minutes of the governing board and all committees with board delegated powers shall contain:

a. The names of the persons who disclosed or otherwise were found to have a financial interest in connection with an actual or possible conflict of interest, the nature of the financial interest, any action taken to determine whether a conflict of interest was present, and the governing boards or committee's decision as to whether a conflict of interest in fact existed.

b. The names of the persons who were present for discussions and votes relating to the transaction or arrangement, the content of the discussion, including any alternatives to the

proposed transaction or arrangement, and a record of any votes taken in connection with the proceedings.

Compensation

Each director, principal officer and member of a committee with governing board delegated powers shall annually sign a statement which affirms such person:

a.   Has received a copy of the bylaws

b.   Has received a copy of the conflicts of interest policy,

c.   Has read and understands the policy

d.   Has agreed to comply with the policy, and understands the organization is charitable and in order to maintain its federal tax exemption it must engage primarily in activities which accomplish one or more of its tax-exempt purposes.

Periodic Reviews

To ensure the organization operates in a manner consistent with charitable purposes and does not engage in activities that could jeopardize its tax-exempt status, periodic reviews shall be conducted. The periodic reviews shall, at a minimum, include the following subjects:

a. Whether compensation arrangements and benefits are reasonable, based on competent survey information and the result of arm's length bargaining.

b. Whether partnerships, joint ventures, and arrangements with management organizations conform to the organization's written policies, are properly recorded, reflect reasonable investment or payments for goods and services, further charitable purposes and do not result in increment, impermissible private benefit or in an excess benefit transaction.

Use of Outside Experts

When conducting the periodic reviews as provided for in Article VII, the Organization may, but need not, use outside advisors. If outside experts are used, their use shall not relieve the governing board of its responsibility for ensuring periodic reviews are conducted.

Security of all Funds

All funds coming into the organization shall be the responsibility of three parties:

1. Logging of checks and monetary donations

2. Deposits to the bank

3. Reconciliation of bank accounts

James 2:12(KJV)

"so speak ye, and so do, as they that shall be judged by the law of liberty."

Tip: Make sure your board members signs acknowledgement of receipt of Bylaws.

ACKNOWLEDGEMENT OF RECEIPT OF BYLAWS FORM
(Example)

I understand that I am expected to read the entire manual and that any questions about the manual or its contents should be directed to my supervisor or human resources department.

I understand that it is my responsibility to comply with the policies and procedures in this manual and all revisions made to it.

I understand that _____ reserves the right to change, modify, suspend or abolish any or all of the policies, benefits, rules, and regulations contained or described in the manual as it deems appropriate at any time, with or without notice.

I acknowledge that neither the manual nor its contents are an express or implied contract regarding my employment at _____

I further understand that my employment/volunteer is an at-will basis and _____ can terminate my employment/volunteer status at any time, with or without cause, and with or without notice.

Please keep a signed copy for your personal records and submit a signed copy to your human resources director for your file. Your human resources director will submit your signed acknowledgment to the Office of the Child Protection Officer.

I further understand that no one is authorized to provide any employee or employees/volunteers with an employment contract or special arrangement concerning terms or conditions of employment/volunteer unless the contract or agreement is in writing and signed by the Human Resources Director and Executive Director.

Signature_____Date_____Volunteer_____

Congratulations! You have completed your bylaws and your board has agreed.

I Call You Friend - Listening Prayer

John 15:13-17 (KJV)

"Greater love hath no man than this, that a man lay down his life for his friends."

Ye are my friends, if ye do whatsoever I command you.

CHAPTER 6
HOW TO BE 'BOARD FRIENDLY'

W hen seeking board members, we tend to ask our family members and friends. Although this may seem logical, it is not best practice. However, family can't make up the majority of your board. A good rule of thumb is to choose a minimum of three board members that are not related to you through family or business ties. While you can have family members or business partners on the board, you'll need to properly disclose that to the IRS according to harborcompliance.com (June 15, 2017 article).

Luke 6:13 (KJV) "And when it was day, he called unto him his disciples: and of them he chose twelve, whom also he named apostles; *They were strangers to one another, and they all had different roles."*

Don't be afraid to meet people and share your vision with them. Ask them to be a part of the mission God has given you.

How to Gain Board Members using the Power of Influence

The 21 Irrefutable Laws of Leadership: book written by John C. Maxwell and published by Thomas Nelson. He quotes: The law of influence states that the greatness of a leader is not measured by the amount of money one makes or position one has, but by the amount of lives one influences. Without influence, you will never be able to lead others. (John Maxwell)

1.   We learn by doing

2.   Only knowledge that is used sticks in your mind.

3.   Don't look merely to acquire information, acquire to form new habits.

4.   Ask yourself how you can apply each suggestion.

5.   Apply these principles to every opportunity.

The Basic Role of Your Board

What's the role of the board of directors of a nonprofit corporation? Great question, **according to the Council of Nonprofit website,** the board of directors has three primary legal duties known as the "**duty of care,**" "**duty of loyalty,**" and "**duty of obedience.**"

- **Duty of Care - *Matthew 25:40 (KJV)*** "Then the King will say, 'I'm telling the solemn truth: Whenever you did one of these things to someone overlooked or ignored, that was me - you did it to me.'"

   Take care of the nonprofit by ensuring prudent use of all assets, including facility, people, and good will.

- **Duty of Loyalty - *Matthew 26:35 (KJV)*** "Peter said unto him, 'Though I should die with thee, yet will I not deny thee.' Likewise, also said all the disciples."

   Ensure that the nonprofit's activities and transactions are, first and foremost, advancing its mission; recognizing and disclose conflicts of interest.

- **Duty of Obedience - *1 Samuel 15:22 (KJV):*** "Has the Lord as great a delight in burnt offerings and sacrifices as in obedience to the voice of the Lord. Behold, to obey is better than sacrifice, and to heed is better than the fat of rams."

  Ensure that the nonprofit obeys applicable laws and regulations, follows its own bylaws, and adheres to its stated corporate purposes/mission.

What Does it Mean to be a Board Member of a Nonprofit?

- The board of directors is the governing body of a nonprofit. Individuals who sit on the board are responsible for overseeing the organization's activities. Board members meet periodically to discuss and vote on the affairs of the organization. At a minimum, an annual meeting must occur with all board members present.

When looking for your board member, keep in mind it's not about you; it's about the mission and the purpose of your nonprofit organization. Here are a few of my proven strategies to get you started:

1. **Simply Ask.**

   How this perspective can be of assistance to the organization.

2. **Why?**

   Why are they passionate about the mission?

3. **After the why, then ask how?**

   How can you help the mission?

Example: My sisters' children were placed in foster care at birth. My thoughts were, "What would happen to them when they reached the age of 18? Where would they go? Who would guide them in their young adulthood?" My strategy is my story, sharing with them long-term direction the organization uses as an advantage in allocating resources to fulfill the mission promised.

4. Don't forget to define your what.

Knowing the **why,** and **how,** is only part of it. It's important to define your **what** as well. That's most easily discovered through learning what operational programs your organization will implement to fulfill its mission. Some questions associated with this might be:

- What does my organization do?

- What resources are needed to support the programs, and how are those obtained?

- What regulations exist to monitor the work?

- What measurable outcomes does the organization generate?

- What determines whether the organization is accomplishing results?

- What does the organization still want to accomplish?

What organizational level determines resources, competency, methodology, and milestones that will assist in better understanding the needs and goals of a successful organization?

5. Why a Board?

Board service is typically designed to be the expression of the owner's mission for the ministry. As a non-profit, there are no owners in a legal sense; the broader community is likely the owner from a moral perspective. The board has a primary responsibility of representing the broader community and making decisions based on what is best for the organization.

Another way to think about this primary role is that true governance represents the community one-step-down. Board members act as the stewards for the collective. A strong board understands this and makes that understanding clear through a formal written policy statement, which includes a job description for the board as a group before breaking down roles on an individual level.

Keep the main focus where it belongs, on the mission and the board members as guardians of the community and stewards for the ministry organization. Before assigning positions, create a well thought out list of key duties and responsibilities.

Be prepared to share your vision and mission when asking perspective people to join your mission.

Tip: **Here is where your elevator pitch comes in handy.**

Board Members according to the Bible

Proverbs 18:24 (ASV)

"He that maketh many friends [doeth it] to his own destruction; But there is a friend that sticketh closer than a brother."

Congratulations! You are on your way to finding board members who have a passion for the mission of your nonprofit.

Will You Declare? - Listening Prayer

Ezekiel 12:25 (KJV)

"For I am the LORD: I will speak, and the word that I shall speak shall come to pass; it shall be no more prolonged: for in your days, O rebellious house, will I say the word, and will perform it, saith the Lord GOD."

I encourage you to stand on and speak the word of God, no matter what it looks like. Trust Him to provide and meet all of your needs for the mission He has called you to.

CHAPTER 7

SPEAK IT

I am my elevator speech, and you should be yours as well.

What is an Elevator Pitch?

Be ready to seize this opportunity to share your nonprofit ministry at any given moment. Imagine you just entered an elevator with a potential board member or sponsor. You have less than 60 seconds to explain your nonprofit ministry mission and what makes it important. An elevator pitch is just that, a persuasive speech that you use to create interest in your ministry. A good elevator pitch should last no longer than a short elevator ride of 20 to 30 seconds **according to mindtools.com.**

How Do I Write My Elevator Pitch?

An elevator pitch should include a basic description of your nonprofit ministry and a description of what makes it unique and special.

For example: "Did You Know 25,000 youth will age out of the foster care system with no place to call home? My name is Crystal R. Durham. I am the founder of Ninety Days of Love Crisis

Center, Inc., and I would love to have coffee and share our mission with you."

Get right to the point of your mission.

Elevator Pitch Scripture

Mark 11:23 (KJV)

"For verily I say unto you, That whosoever shall say unto this mountain, Be thou removed, and be thou cast into the sea; and shall not doubt in his heart, but shall believe that those things which he saith shall come to pass; he shall have whatsoever he saith"

Congratulations! You created your elevator pitch.

Are You Equipped? - Listening Prayer

Ephesian 4:11-12 (MGS)

"Filled earth with his gifts. He handed out gifts of apostle, prophet, evangelist, and pastor-teacher to train Christians in skilled servant work, working within Christ's body, the church,"

CHAPTER 8
WHO'S IN CHARGE?

Board Members Positions

I was just like you when it came to assigning positions for my board members. I was clueless. However, what I did have was the power to share my story. That is all you need. Sharing your passion with others and all that God has called you to is very inspiring and will draw others in.

When you open up and let people in, you will find out just how many good people there are in the world and how they are eagerly seeking to be a part of something bigger than themselves. So, I encourage you to be brave, be courageous, be inspiring, and allow God to do the rest. Get out of your comfort zone and meet people. I met the secretary of my board out on a date night with my husband. I met one of my board members at a women's group meeting. I met another one working my part-time job while collecting coats for our Annual Christmas Coat Drive, and guess what? You guessed it. That individual donated over 10 coats and $150.00 to our nonprofit. Opening up and sharing with others what God has called you to do can never do any harm. It can only bring good.

Psalms 91:11-12 (MSG)

"He ordered his angels to guard you wherever you go. If you stumble, they'll catch you; their job is to keep you from falling.

We have not because we ask not.

How Do I Build a Role Based Board?

Before you undertake the responsibility for developing your nonprofit ministry's board, I strongly recommend defining the need and clarifying the responsibilities of each potential board member before you begin the recruitment process. Recruiting board members based on the needs or your organization first and bringing clarity to the roles you seek to fill is a good strategy, which shows your leadership to future board members.

Chosen Board Member According to Scriptures

Matthew 4:19-20 (MSG)

"Jesus said to them 'Come with me. I'll make a new kind of fisherman out of you. I'll show you how to catch men and women instead of perch and bass.' They didn't ask questions, but simply dropped their nets and followed."

Do I Need A President and a CEO?

"This is such a commonly asked question when structuring the governance and management of a nonprofit corporation. Do nonprofits need to maintain both of these positions? And how does an Executive Director fit into this equation? **According to Councilofnonprofit.org here are some differences.**"

Directors vs. Officers

It's important to first distinguish between directors (board members) and officers. Generally, directors have no inherent individual authority or power. Their authority and power is exercised collectively as a board. Officers, on the other hand, are delegated with certain authority and power, which may be spelled out in a position or job description.

Officers

State laws generally require that a corporation have certain officers. The Nonprofit Public Benefit Corporation Law (the "NPBC Law") requires such corporations to have the following officers:

- **A president or a chair of the board;**

- **A secretary**

- **A treasurer or a chief financial officer.**

The NPBC Law does not explicitly require that any officer be a director, though it may be understood that only a director can serve as chair of the board. Regardless, it is relatively common for all-volunteer organizations to elect officers from among the directors. It is also common for large organizations with employees to hire certain officers (like a CEO and CFO) who are not directors.

Who is the CEO?

The NPBC Law provides that the president, or if there is no president, the chair of the board, is the general manager and chief executive officer of the corporation, unless otherwise provided in the articles or bylaws. Accordingly, if a nonprofit corporation's articles and bylaws are silent on the issue and assuming the corporation has a president, the president will be the CEO. Similarly, if the corporation's governing documents are silent on the issue and the corporation doesn't have a president, the chair of the board will be the CEO.

Duties of the CEO

While the duties of any officer are generally those spelled out in a position description, often contained in the bylaws, the CEO is generally thought to have certain inherent responsibilities and authority associated with an executive in charge of the management of a corporation, subject only to the authority of the board (but not of any individual director) or executive committee.

Should a Nonprofit Have Both a President and Chair of the Board?

There is no one answer that will fit all organizations. However, let's look at how a board might reach an answer based on specific circumstances:

- In volunteer organizations, there is probably no need to have both a president and a chair of the board unless there is intent to select each position independently. If the long-term plan is to have one volunteer lead the organization and the board, it seems unnecessary to provide both titles to the individual. In such case, president may be the preferable position title as it suggests a role beyond presiding overboard meetings. Nevertheless, the bylaws might provide for the option of electing a chair of the board, should it later become desirable to have a different individual in such role.

- For organizations with paid employees, there may be advantages to having a compensated CEO and a separate volunteer chair of the board. **In such case, the CEO is often provided the title of president.** Because the

CEO serves at the pleasure of the board, and typically has their performance reviewed and compensation determined by the board, separating the CEO and chair of the board functions by assigning them to different individuals can help avoid the major conflicts of interest that would otherwise be possessed by someone with both responsibilities. In some cases, however, having one individual serve as both CEO and chair of the board may be okay despite the conflict of interest. **For example**, this may be true where a founder being compensated to act as the CEO is also the champion and clear leader of the board, which lacks another director ability to fulfill their responsibilities of board chair. Lack of developing additional leadership can lead to the problems. From a legal perspective, this may reflect the other directors' breach of trust duties due to the lack of exercising independent judgment.

As I stated, you only need **three board** members to file for your 501c3 tax exempt.

Here are the duties of all three: Duties of the President

If the president is the CEO, the position description will be reflective of such authority and its accompanying duties and responsibilities. If the president is not the CEO, the nonprofit should make sure that there is a clear action of describing between the positions and relative authority and responsibilities of president and CEO. For purposes of the following sample description of duties (probably more suited to a small to medium-sized nonprofit), I'll assume that the **president is the CEO** and does not preside over meetings of the board.

Description

The president is the general manager and chief executive officer of this corporation and is subject to the control of the board, general supervision, direction and control of the business, activities and officers (other than the chair of the board) of this corporation. The president has the general powers and duties of management usually vested in the office of president and general manager of a corporation and such other powers and duties as may be prescribed by the board. Among other things, the president shall be responsible for:

- Ensuring the organization's activities are compliant and in furtherance of its mission.

- Leading, managing, and developing the organization's employees, volunteers, and organizational culture.

- Developing, implementing, monitoring, and assessing the organization's programs (including their impact).

- Developing, implementing, monitoring, and assessing sound and compliant financial management practices (including budgeting).

- Developing, implementing, monitoring, and assessing sound and compliant fundraising practices.

- Developing, informing, and supporting the board and the board committees to carry out their governance functions.

- Partnering with the chair of the board to help ensure the board's directives, policies, and resolutions are carried out.

- Working with the development staff and chair of the board in cultivating and soliciting major foundation grants and individual gifts.

- Developing and maintaining beneficial relationships with donors, funders, supporters, collaborators, allies, vendors, and other stakeholders.

- Ensuring effective external communications about the organization and its mission, priorities, importance, programs, and activities.

- Championing the organization and advocating its mission to internal and external stakeholders.

- Keeping informed and the organization's leadership informed of significant developments and changes in the internal and external environment.

- Leading the organization's planning processes.

- Ensuring legal compliance (including all required filings) and sound risk management practices.

Duties of the Chair of the Board

Description

The chair of the board shall, if present, preside at all meetings of the board and the executive committee, act as a liaison between the board and the president to help ensure the board's directives and resolutions are carried out, and exercise and perform such other powers and duties as may be from time to time prescribed by the board. More specifically, the chair of the board shall be responsible for:

- Leading the board and executive committee to carry out its governance functions.

- Ensuring the board has approved policies to help ensure sound and compliant governance and management of the organization.

- Partnering with the president/CEO to lead the development and refinement of impact metrics.

- Assessing the performance of the board and its committees.

- Assuring ongoing recruitment, development, and contributions of board members.

- Partnering with the president/CEO to help ensure the board's directives, policies, and resolutions are carried out.

- Working with the president/CEO in cultivating and soliciting major foundation grants and individual gifts.

- Coordinating an annual performance review of the president/CEO.

- Setting priorities and creating agendas for meetings of the board and executive committee.

- Presiding over meetings of the board and executive committee.

- Serving as an ambassador of the organization and advocating its mission to internal and external stakeholders.

If the chair of the board is the CEO, the position description will be reflective of such authority and its accompanying duties and responsibilities (see sample description of president's duties above). In such case, if the nonprofit also has an executive director, it should make sure that there is a clear delineation between the two positions and their relative authority and responsibilities.

Duties of a Secretary

The secretary of a nonprofit organization plays a critical role in fostering communication and ensuring proper management and utilization of important organizational records. Generally, an organization's bylaws will set the duties of the secretary; however, duties may change from time to time as may be assigned by the board. A secretary will be most useful to an organization when his or her role is shaped to meet the unique structure and needs of the organization, rather than filling a standard job description.

Typically, the secretary should be equipped to handle the following matters:

Communication is a Primary Role of the Secretary

The secretary of the corporation is an active conduit for communication between the board, management, and members (if any), by giving proper notice of any meetings and timely distribution of materials such as agendas and meeting minutes. The secretary should be knowledgeable of the organization's records and related materials and should be able to provide advice and resources to the board on relevant topics, such as particular governance matters being addressed at a meeting or a new amendment to state corporate law, for example. The secretary should aim to be helpful to the board as they discharge their fiduciary duties.

Scheduling, Notice, and Materials

The secretary is tasked with knowing and complying with notice requirements and scheduling meetings to accommodate the directors. Notice requirements can be particularly important. The secretary is responsible for scheduling board meetings and should ensure an adequate number of meetings are held per year, in accordance with the organization's bylaws. Generally, a board can more efficiently and effectively hold a board meeting when the secretary prepares and sends meeting materials far enough in advance of the meeting for each director to review such materials, correct any errors, and prepare questions and comments.

Minutes of Meetings

The secretary is also charged with recording minutes of meetings. Minutes are an important organizational document and provide a memorialized chronology of key information such as board actions, elections of officers or directors, and certain reports from committees and staff. Meeting minutes can have vital legal significance in an IRS examination and as evidence in courts if, for example, someone challenges the validity of certain actions or positions. The secretary should be well-equipped to record accurate minutes and be aware and sensitive to any special or confidential information discussed at a meeting.

Maintenance of Corporate Records

As the custodian of the organization's records, the secretary is responsible for maintaining accurate documentation and meeting legal requirements, such as annual filing deadlines. It may be helpful for the secretary to have a calendar of filing deadlines, which may include a filing with the corporation's Secretary of State, the Attorney General, the state tax agency, and the IRS. The secretary is responsible for reviewing and updating documents as necessary and ensuring all documents are safely stored and readily accessible for inspection by directors and/or members. In California, an organization's articles of incorporation and bylaws, as amended to date, should be available at the corporation's principal office for inspection. Additionally, it is required that a nonprofit's exemption application and past three annual returns with the IRS are available for public inspection.

The secretary position has wide-ranging responsibilities, requiring much more than simply being present at all board meetings. These duties likely will increase if the corporation has a voting membership structure, which requires additional notice procedures and voting. Each board should carefully consider how the secretary can best serve their organization. If you don't recruit any other board members, these are the most important ones to have.

Treasurer Role

The treasurer generally is charged with overseeing the management and reporting of the organization's finances. In a large nonprofit with accounting staff and a chief financial officer, the treasurer will usually head a finance committee that reports to the board of directors. He or she focuses mainly on reviewing internally prepared financial reports and evaluating financial policies and procedures.

By contrast, in a smaller organization with no internal accounting staff, the treasurer may need to get down in the trenches — writing checks and making deposits, managing and safeguarding funds and maintaining financial integrity. Where applicable, he or she might also oversee outside bookkeepers, tax preparers, fundraisers and investment advisors.

Regardless of the organization's size, the treasurer typically shepherds the development of the not-for-profit's financial policies, such as those for investing, borrowing and cash reserves. And he or she presents regular treasurer's reports to the board of directors. These can range from a simple "dashboard" to more detailed information.

Specific Areas of Concern

The treasurer must cover several different areas. Depending on the organization's resources, the treasurer's degree of involvement will vary. He or she might take on the following duties personally or just observe carefully and provide specific instructions to assure that staff is handling them appropriately.

Budget

The annual budget is the financial map of the organization's goals and how it plans to achieve them in the upcoming year. The treasurer should present the budget for board approval, being realistic about both revenues and expenses. He or she should also review current reports frequently for differences between actual and budgeted figures and determine the reasons for those discrepancies.

Financial Reports

The board relies on the treasurer to provide timely and accurate financial information to support its decision-making. In addition to financial statements, the treasurer might supply information on financial ratios and trends that describe the organization's current and projected financial status.

Compliance

Complying with relevant laws and tax regulations is a top priority for the treasurer. They must also work with your CPA and keep a calendar of reporting and filing deadlines to avoid late fees, penalties and the damage they can bring.

Risk Management

In addition, the treasurer should coordinate with your CPA and insurance agent to regularly perform assessments that identify and mitigate risks to the organization's assets, data and confidential information. You might have risks, for instance, related to the use of volunteers in money-handling positions. Mitigation could include internal controls designed to prevent and identify fraud.

Audit

Once your nonprofit reaches a certain size, its books should be audited annually by an independent CPA. The treasurer should review the results and recommendations — asking questions where appropriate — and present them to your board.

The Right Person for the Job

You need to be selective about candidates' qualifications. Looking at such responsibilities, it's clear that not just anyone can function well in the treasurer position. For starters, the treasurer must confirm that they are knowledgeable in financial literacy, including a thorough understanding of the various financial reports and accounting practices used by nonprofits. They also should possess an attention to detail, adhere to deadlines, have patience, curiosity and recordkeeping skills. The treasurer needs the motivation to make, and keep up with, the timely commitment required for the job. Having people skills is a plus for the treasure as well. A passion for the nonprofit ministry also is valuable.

The Bottom Line

The specific duties treasurers perform will differ, depending on the nonprofit ministry's circumstances. Without a qualified treasurer performing proper oversight, your nonprofit ministry's finances will be in jeopardy. Investing in the right person will pay off in the long run.

Congratulations! You now know the positions of your immediate board members to govern your organization.

Now, getting board members and placing them in position and engaged is one thing, keeping them engaged is another thing. I was able to gain some great insight from several different articles from different sites, and I have been able to keep my board engaged over the years. **Boardontrack.org was one of them, and here is some of the information I found useful for our nonprofit ministry.**

How to Increase Board Engagement?

The type of board members your ministry needs are the type of people that have full schedules with important goals to accomplish. I say this because of the book of **Matthew 4:18 (NIV)** "Jesus was walking beside the Sea of Galilee, he saw two brothers, called Peter and his brother Andrew. They were casting a net into the lake, for they were fishermen. 'Come, follow me,' Jesus said, 'and I will make you fishers of men.' At once they left their nets and followed him."

Jesus founded His board while they were working. Nonprofits often struggle with how to engage their board members, in ways that can increase their passion for their nonprofit ministry.

Here are simple ways to increase board member engagement:

1. Encourage your board members to volunteer in the ministry; I do this at every event. This will create an emotional connection for them to see the impact your nonprofit ministry is making.

2. At your first board meeting, set clear expectations.

3. Start and end your board meeting on time.

4. Make sure each board member is clear on financial contributing.

5. Make evaluations a priority.

6. Meet for Dinner/Lunch.

7. Develop an annual/clear budget.

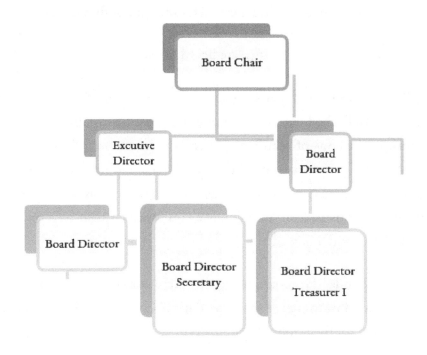

Example

You should have a board in place and hold a board meeting before filing your ministry 501c3. This is a best practice.

Breaking Bread - Listening Prayer

1 Corinthians 14:26 (MSG)

"So here's what I want you to do. When you gather for worship, each one of you be prepared with something that will be useful for all: Sing a hymn, teach a lesson, tell a story, lead a prayer, provide an insight."

CHAPTER 9
HAVE A SEAT AT THE BOARD TABLE

This is one thing I had to really work on when I first got started. It's hard to build relationships with your board members when they have their own lives and live in different areas. At times, I still struggle when it comes to staying connected. Here's my suggestion. At your first board meeting, be as open and welcoming as possible. Remember, it's not about you, rather it is about your mission, and your mission must be the topic of discussion.

How to Prepare for your First Board Meeting

The first step is preparing a budget for the board meeting.

Have a sign in sheet to take attendance or name tags.

Preparing for your first nonprofit ministry board meeting can be stressful, so planning it out can actually improve your nonprofit ministry's overall performance.

When your board meeting is run effectively, it will be worth every minute you spent planning it. In many cases, it can move your ministry closer to its goals, through sheer support and encouragement to and from your board members.

Board Meeting Sign in Sheet (Example)

January 1, 2020

Agenda Meeting Minutes		
START TIME: 3:30PM (EST)	END TIME: 5:30PM (EST)	DATE:
TYPE OF MEETING		
FACILITATO R		
ATTENDEES:		
Agenda Topics: Meet & Greet, New Volunteers, Financials, Fundraisers Gala, NPO to NPO 5K Awareness Walk 2019		
1HR		PRESENTER: CRYSTAL R. DURHAM
DISCUSSION		

CONCLUSIO NS	
(15 MIN) WRAP UP	
ASSIGNED	
PREPARER	

Name	Email Address

1. **Prepare the board meeting agenda in advance** - Prepare your nonprofit board meeting agenda at least a month before the board meeting. Send out an announcement to all board members along with the agenda for the upcoming meeting at least 7 days prior. Make sure to include any financial statements, reports, and other documents in the email, so that your board members have enough time to familiarize themselves with

the information before the meeting. Make sure the information is well-organized and easy to read.

2. **Make sure the board meeting agenda is strategic -** Plan a strategy and have a checklist of topics to be discussed in your meeting.

3. **Make sure the board meeting agenda is mission-focused -** Make achieving the mission of the nonprofit ministry more important than any other items on your board meeting agenda. When you keep your ministry board meeting agenda mission-focused, it keeps your meeting on the right track. You may even write your nonprofit mission statement on the top of the agenda so that everyone is constantly reminded of it. You could also share stories you may have received in an email to encourage your board members. This helps the board stay connected to your ministry's purpose and mission.

4. **Here are 5 Tips I have used in our nonprofit ministry, from Inc.com, to help ensure a successful first board meeting. I am sure it will help you as well.**

1. Be confident

2. Keep control of the meeting

3. Know who will be at the table

4. Prepare to discuss future growth

5. Get expectations from your board

4. Start and end your nonprofit board meeting on time - This is a pet peeve of mine - starting late and ending late. It will become clear to those late comers. When your nonprofit ministry starts late because its members are late, this often results in meetings constantly being pushed back, and your board members arriving later and later. I can't stress this enough - Always start your meetings on time!

First meetings may go a little longer but try to limit the length of meetings to two hours or less, if possible, especially if you're holding the meeting in the evening. If you must go longer than two hours, take a break. Offering refreshments before the meeting begins is a good way to maintain the flow. Also, when you start and end your nonprofit ministry board meetings on time, it shows your board members you value their time.

5. Make the meeting about decisions and not updates - Your board members are one of your greatest resources. Your ministry board members should be doing at least 80% of the talking during the meeting. That talk should focus mostly on decisions and strategic discussions, not updates **(except for the absolutely necessary ones).**

Try not to overload or consume your board with too much information. It can cause them to have difficulty making time for genuine dialogue and decision making on important issues. Let the main focus be the main focus, which is the mission, and discussions about long-term strategic goals and how the board can add to them.

The secretary should seek ways to minimize large information downloads and reporting. Instead, utilize an agenda for approval of routine items such as minutes, contracts, vetted policies, etc. The types of items that appear on a consent agenda are non-controversial items or routine items that are discussed at every meeting.

6. Take Board Meeting Minutes - Very few people enjoy the idea of taking, preparing, distributing, and/or reviewing meeting minutes. However, if done appropriately for your nonprofit's needs, meeting minutes can be a very useful tool in keeping your board focused on the task at hand. Distribute board meeting minutes to all meeting participants within 24 hours after each board meeting. This ensures action steps are fresh and solidified in everyone's mind, and it shows your board members you care.

To make the process smoother, get a copy of the meeting agenda and use it as a guide for taking notes and preparing the minutes – with the order and numbering of items on the minutes of meeting matching those of the agenda. To keep the board engaged, highlight actions and the person designated for completing them.

Here are a few tips to make minute-taking easier:

Record decisions or notes on action items in your outline as soon as they occur.

- Ask for clarification if necessary

- Be brief with your notes; don't go into too many details in your notes.

- Don't use people's names except for motions and seconds, when it is needed.

- Highlight to indicate strategic action plans and who will serve as the lead.

- Vote on having some type of recording device to serve as an excellent backup for your notes.

- Keep the meeting minutes safely filed away.

Use your meeting minutes to prepare the next board meeting agenda.

7. Get a Good Nonprofit Board Chair - Your nonprofit ministry board meeting agenda is your most important tool for running effective nonprofit board meetings. However, an agenda can only do so much. A crucial part of a successful board meeting is a good nonprofit board chair. So, what are the qualities of a good board chair?

To be effective, they need to have essential knowledge and understanding of your nonprofit's governance principles. They also need to have experience and knowledge of your industry and operations. Besides that, board chairs must have the social skills and organizational skills to run a board meeting efficiently and effectively.

Board chairs need to be able to deal with multiple personalities and a variety of social situations. They should ideally be open, in order to hear all arguments and allow opinions to flow. They must also be firm, in order to facilitate the agenda and make sure everything runs smoothly and on time. A board chair should also gently steer discussions and recognize those who contribute good suggestions. It is also their task to not let one or two board members dominate every board meeting.

Additional Tips

- **Post an acronym chart -** Make a poster of frequently used external and internal acronyms and post it on the wall of every meeting.

- **Distribute name tags at every meeting** - Having name tags eliminates potential embarrassing situations for your board members.

- **Share some food -** Having a pot of soup or a plate of cookies, spreads, and crackers is good for setting a positive atmosphere. This works very well in helping build a social atmosphere that cultivates trust and the ability of the group to work together. However, be careful with board dinners! It may turn into something other than a board meeting.

- **Measure Board Effectiveness** - Do this by offering meeting evaluation forms after each board session to get feedback on whether the meeting successfully achieved its goals or have the chair or president check in for *satisfaction checks.*

- **Thank your board** - Both the board chair and the President should send a *thank you* email to each board member and every member who participated. The email should be waiting for them as soon as they arrive home or sit down at their desks first thing the following workday.

Appoint a Temporary Chair and Secretary (to take minutes)

- In order to conduct a meeting, you will need someone to chair the meeting and someone to record the meeting. So, your first order of business is to designate these people. This should be motioned and voted on.

Example of How to make Motion when Adopting Bylaws, Board Members, etc....

Motion: I move that _____ be appointed as temporary chair for this meeting. This motion requires a *second* before discussion about the motion can begin. Once the discussion is complete, a vote should follow to select the temporary chair.

Motion: I move that _____ be appointed as temporary secretary for this meeting. This motion requires a *second* before discussion about the motion can begin. Once the discussion is complete a vote should follow to select the temporary secretary.

- At this point, the temporary chairperson will conduct the meeting and the temporary secretary shall record the minutes.

- Report on Filing of articles of incorporation

- Your articles of incorporation should have already been filed and approved by your state. The chair of the meeting should report to the board that this has been done. At this point the board needs to make the articles of Incorporation part of the official record.

  Motion: I make a motion to direct the secretary of this corporation to make a copy of the signed and certified articles of incorporation and place them in a corporate binder to be kept at our principal office. This motion requires a *second* before discussion about the motion can begin. Once the discussion is complete, a vote should occur to accept the motion. The secretary should record this motion and the results of the vote.

Adoption of Bylaws

- At this point, the chair should present the board with the organization's bylaws. Before discussion can begin someone must make a motion to adopt the bylaws. It is a good idea to email a copy of the bylaws to all meeting attendees prior to the first official meeting.

  Motion: I make a motion to adopt the presented bylaws as the bylaws of this organization. This motion requires a *second* before discussion can continue. Once seconded, any amendments (changes) can be introduced and voted on. Once the discussion is complete a vote should occur and be recorded by the secretary.

- Appointment of Officers

- Now that you have accepted articles of incorporation and approved your bylaws, it is time to officially elect your board officers.

Motion: I nominate _____ to the office of president of this organization. This motion requires a *second* before the discussion about the motion can begin. Once all nominations have been received, you can proceed with a vote in accordance with your bylaws. This should be recorded by the secretary.

Repeat this motion for the vice-president, treasurer and secretary. After completion of all the voting, the new officers should take their positions and relieve the temporary officers of their duties.

- **Note:** It is okay to have one person serve in multiple offices on your board, though many states will restrict which offices can be held by the same person. For instance, it is common for states to require that the office of president and secretary not be held by the same person. Check with your state filing office to see what conditions apply to you.

Designate Principal Office

Most states require that a principal office be designated when you file your articles of incorporation. Now that you have an official board, you should confirm the location of your principal office.

Motion: I make a motion that the principal office of this organization be located at _____. This motion requires a *second* before discussion about the motion can begin. Once the discussion is complete, a vote should occur and be recorded by the secretary.

- **Optional Agenda Items**

- **Open a Corporate Bank Account**

At some point, you will need to open a bank account for your organization. It is good practice to make any financial related decisions in a motion. If your board is ready to open a bank account, then proceed with the following motion.

Motion: I make a motion to authorize the president (or other officer) to apply for an employee identification number and open a corporate account at the _____ bank.

File for Tax Exemption

If you plan to become a 501©3 tax exempt organization, then you will need to authorize someone to apply for tax-exempt status as a charitable organization under Section 501(c)3 of the Internal Revenue Code.

Motion: I make a motion to authorize _____ to apply for tax-exempt status as a charitable organization under Section 501(c)(3) of the Internal Revenue Code.

File Requires State Reports

Once your organization has its first official meeting, many states require an initial report or registration to be filed. Check with your state to see which reports need to be filed.

Motion: I move to authorize _____ to file all reports and registration statements required by our state statutes for new corporations. These reports/filings should include_____.

- This wraps up your first nonprofit ministry board meeting and everyone coming to the board table. Always make coming together be centered on the mission and the purpose of your nonprofit ministry, keeping in mind **Luke 22:14-19.**

Luke 22:14-15 (MSG)

When it was time, he sat down, all the apostles with him, and said, "You've no idea how much I have looked forward to eating this Passover meal with you before I enter my time of suffering."

Board Roles

When looking for your board, look at what skills, talent and experience it will require to take your nonprofit ministry to the next level, and identify which roles you need going forward. Here is an example of a chart to note each role you need for future growth based on the skill or experience in your nonprofit ministry.

Names of the Board Members in their appropriate roles form (example)

Director	Community Lead	Professional

Board Agreement Form Example

As a board member of _____, I am fully committed and dedicated to the mission and have pledged to carry out this mission. I understand that my duties and responsibilities include the following:

I am fiscally responsible, with other board directors, for the organization, I will know what our budget is and take an active part in reviewing, approving, and monitoring the budget and fundraising to meet it.

I know I am legally responsible for knowing and overseeing the implementation of policies and programs.

I accept the bylaws and operating principles manual and understand that I am morally responsible for the health and well-being of this organization.

I will give what is suitable for me as a donation. I may give this as a one-time donation each year, or I may pledge to give a certain amount several times during the year.

I will actively engage in fundraising for this organization in whatever ways are best suited for me. These may include individual solicitations, undertaking special events, writing mail appeals, and the like; I am making a good faith agreement to do my best and to raise as much money as I can.

I will actively promote _____ and encourage and support its staff.

I will attend board meetings, be available for phone consultation, and serve on at least one committee. If I am not able to meet my obligations as a board director, I will offer my resignation.

In signing this document, I understand that no quotas are being set and that no rigid standards of measurement and achievement are being formed. Every board of director is making a statement of faith about every other board director. We trust each other to carry out the above agreement to the best of our ability.

Signed_____Date_____

Colossians 4:2 (MSG) "*D*evote yourselves to prayer with an attitude of thanksgiving."

Congratulations! You have completed your first board meeting!

Are You in Position? - Listening Prayer

Romans 12:6-8 (MSG)

"Let's just go ahead and be what we were made to be, without enviously or pride fully comparing ourselves with each other, or trying to be something we aren't. If you preach, just preach God's Message, nothing else; if you help, just help, don't take over; if you teach, stick to your teaching; if you give encouraging guidance, be careful that you don't get bossy; if you're put in charge, don't manipulate; if you're called to give aid to people in distress, keep your eyes open and be quick to respond; if you work with the disadvantaged, don't let yourself get irritated with them or depressed by them. Keep a smile on your face."

CHAPTER 10
BOARD MEMBERS POSITION AND DESCRIPTION

According to Boardsource.org, here are board members position and descriptions.

Director of Development Position Description

Position Summary:

The Director of Development is responsible for planning, organizing, and directing all of _____'s fundraising including, the major gifts program, annual fund, planned giving, special events and capital campaigns. The director works closely with the executive director and the board of directors in all development and fundraising endeavors.

Qualifications:

- Must embrace the mission of _____

- Must have strong interpersonal and writing skills

- Must have knowledge and experience in fund raising techniques, particularly major gift fundraising

- Must possess the skills to work with and motivate staff, board members and other volunteers

- Must have the desire to get out of the office and build external relationships

- Must be a "self-starter" and goal driven to initiate donor visits and fundraising calls

- Must be organized and exhibit "follow through" on tasks and goals.

- Must display a positive attitude, show concern for people and community, demonstrate presence, self-confidence, common sense and good listening ability

- Must have a bachelor's degree

- Must have 5 years minimum experience in professional fundraising

ACTUAL JOB RESPONSIBILITIES:

1. Must meet prospective donors and supporters on a continual basis to establish effective communications with them

2. Must grow a major gifts program; including identification, cultivation and solicitation of major donors

3. Must oversee grant seeking; including research, proposal writing, and reporting requirements

4. Must build the planned giving program with a focus on deferred gifts such as bequest expectancies

5. Must direct the annual fund program, including mailings and annual fundraising drives

6. Must direct capital campaigns and other major fundraising drives

7. Must coordinate fund raising special events

8. Must direct employee fundraising drives

9. Must oversee prospect research

10. Must work closely with _____, the executive director, and board of directors.

11. Must make public appearances/accept speaking engagements to share information about the _____ with the community

12. Must hold staff board development committee meetings

13. Must oversee fundraising database and tracking systems

14. Must supervise and collaborate with other fundraising staff

15. Must oversee creation of publications to support fund raising activities

16. Must maintain gift recognition programs

17. Must demonstrate professional conduct at all times

18. Must perform other related duties as requested

Grant Writer Position Description

The grant writer is a part time position that reports directly to the vice president of development and public relations. The grant writer will be responsible for researching, writing and coordinating the grant application process. In addition, they will manage proposals and maintain a donor database.

The grant writer duties will include, but are not limited to:

- Writing high-quality grant proposal narratives, applications, and supporting documents

- Researching, collecting data, and writing grants

- Work with department managers to compile financials and data

- Manage the proposal submission process to ensure timely submission of all required materials

- Develop and maintain a proposal calendar

- Coordinate and follow-up on the progress of submitted proposals

- Develop an annual grants strategy

- Conduct prospect research to identify, cultivate and solicit new grants

- Perform other duties as assigned

Experience/Qualifications:

- Must have a minimum of 2 years of experience in research and grant writing; nonprofit experience is a plus

- Must have a bachelor's degree

- Must be able to write successful grant proposals

- Must have knowledge of NWI and foundations and corporations

- Must be detail-oriented, organized, deadline-driven

- Must have clear, precise and compelling writing skills

- Must be able to effectively communicate

- Must be a motivated, self-starter with the ability to work independently with purpose and accuracy in a fast-paced environment

- Must be Highly proficient in all areas of Microsoft Office to include Outlook, Word, Excel and PowerPoint

Program Manager Position Description/Responsibilities

The program manager is responsible for organizing programs and activities in accordance with the mission and goals of the organization. They are to develop new programs to support the strategic direction of the organization. They are also responsible for creating and managing long-term goals, as well as developing a budget and operating plan for the program.

Program Manager Responsibilities

- Must organize programs and activities in accordance with the mission and goals of the organization

- Must develop new programs to support the strategic direction of the organization

- Must create and manage long-term goals

- Must develop a budget and operating plan for the program

- Must develop an evaluation method to assess program strengths and identify areas for improvement

- Must write program funding proposals to guarantee uninterrupted delivery of services

- Must manage a team with a diverse array of talents and responsibilities

- Must ensure goals are met in all areas; including customer satisfaction, safety, quality and team member performance

- Must implement and manage changes and interventions to ensure project goals are achieved

- Must meet with stakeholders to make communication easy and be transparent regarding project issues and decisions on services

- Must produce accurate and timely reporting of a program's status throughout its life cycle

- Must analyze program risks

- Must work on strategies with the marketing team

Program Manager Requirements

- Must have a bachelor's degree or master's degree in business or related field

- Must have proven experience in program management

- Must have proven stakeholder management skills

- Must have proven experience managing a team

- Must have experience using computers for a variety of tasks

- Must be competent in Microsoft applications; including Word, Excel, and Outlook

- Must have understanding of project management

Chair/Chairperson/President

What should the chief elected officer be called? The least confusing title is chair or chairperson. Many organizations call their chief executive officer *president* to avoid confusion; it makes sense to reserve that title for a staff position and use chair or chairperson for a board position.

Leader of the Board

To function effectively, groups need a leader. A board leader should be approachable and available. He or she should be objective and listen actively. He or she needs to be skilled, knowledgeable about the organization and board practices, a coach, and a mediator. Finally, he or she must be respected in the community. The chair most commonly performs the following functions:

- Serves as the contact point for every board member on board issues

- Sets goals and objectives for the board and ensures that they are met

- Ensures that all board members are involved in committee activities and assigns committee chairs

- Motivates board members to attend meetings

Facilitator of board meetings

One of the trickiest responsibilities of a chair is to run effective and productive board meetings.

Effective meeting facilitators must be able to:

- Create a purposeful agenda in collaboration with the chief executive and follow it.

- Know how to run a less formal and productive meeting.

- Engage each board member in deliberation.

- Control dominating or out-of-line behavior during meetings.

If the board chair is not able to lead an effective meeting, it is better to delegate that task to someone else (such as the vice-chair) rather than risk unproductive or boring meetings.

Should the chair vote?

The chair has the same right to vote as other board members. Some chairs vote while others abstain and vote only to break a tie.

Relationship with the chief executive

Both the chair and the chief executive of the organization need to support, consult, and complement each other. Both have their own responsibilities — the chief manages the operational activities and the chair leads the board. Both share power in their mutual pursuit to advance the mission of the organization. To make this happen, they need to communicate openly and regularly. This partnership needs constant attention. Personalities change but the positions remain. Each partner needs to adapt to and cultivate the working relationship.

Think of the chief executive as the gatekeeper for the staff and the chair as the gatekeeper for the rest of the board. This helps to prevent miscommunication and allows both leaders to stay aware of each other's needs.

Duties of the CEO

While the duties of any officer are generally those spelled out in a position description, often contained in the bylaws, the CEO is generally thought to have certain inherent responsibilities and authority associated with an executive in charge of the management of a corporation, subject only to the authority of the board (but not of any individual director) or executive committee.

Should a Nonprofit Have Both a President and Chair of the Board?

As might be expected, there is no one answer that will fit all organizations. However, the following represents my general opinions on how a board might reach an answer specific to its specific circumstances:

- For organizations with paid employees, there may be advantages to having a compensated CEO and a separate volunteer chair of the board. **In such case, the CEO is often provided the title of president.** Because the CEO serves at the pleasure of the board, and typically has their performance reviewed and pay determined by the board. Separating the CEO and chair of the board functions by assigning them to different individuals can help avoid the major conflicts of interest that would otherwise be possessed by someone with both responsibilities. However, in some cases, having one individual serve as both CEO and chair of the board may be desirable despite the conflict of interest. For example, this may be true where a founder being compensated to act as the CEO is also the champion and clear leader of the board, which lacks another director able to fulfill the responsibilities of a chair of the board. Lack of developing additional leadership can, however, lead to the twin problems of founder's syndrome and a rubber-stamp board. From a legal perspective, this may reflect the other directors' breach of trust duties due to the lack of exercising independent judgment and reasonable care.

Congratulations on building a successful board for your nonprofit organization!

Now that your board is in place, you can now focus on building a volunteer base. Many nonprofits depend on volunteers to help with various projects and having a volunteer base is so important to the growth of your nonprofit ministry organization.

Volunteer Coordinator Position Description

A volunteer coordinator manages all elements of the volunteer force. He or she is typically responsible for recruiting, hiring, and placing volunteers, as well as training and managing them.

Volunteer Coordinator Responsibilities:

- To recruit, train, and supervise new volunteers

- To collect volunteer information, availability and skills, and maintain an up-to-date database

- To use marketing tools such as outreach programs, e-mails, and volunteer databases

- To keep new and existing volunteers informed about the organization and volunteer opportunities

- To match volunteers to opportunities that suit their skill sets, and ensuring they understand their responsibilities and receive the proper training

- To organize training and lead on-the-job training.

- To keep schedules and records of volunteers' work

- To prepare codes of conduct and operating procedures to uphold the organization's values

- To ensure the organization's purpose is conveyed to the public

Volunteer Coordinator Requirements:

- Must have an Associate's in Business Management, Human Resources or a related field

- Must have experience in volunteering and recruitment

- Must have a working knowledge of databases

- Must have excellent communication and interpersonal skills

- Must have excellent organization and team building skills

Community Outreach Coordinator Job Description

A community outreach coordinator should be self-motivated, enthusiastic and community-driven to take on this exciting role. This position requires someone equipped with a positive attitude and readiness to be a team player. Having a talented and professional community outreach coordinator to maintain all community outreach activities will make your organization run smoothly. You will represent the company and work with the management team to develop and implement initiatives that increase company visibility within the surrounding community.

Responsibilities:

- Must maintain a calendar of outreach activities; including community events, workshops, appearances and other communication opportunities

- Must prepare an annual budget for community outreach activities

- Must nurture new and old relationships with collaborative partners

- Must schedule regular outreach exhibitions in the community and educate employees on community responsibility

- Must prepare accurate records and reports on the goals of the fundraising plan

- Must oversee a professional donor management system

- Must assist in the organization of special events; including donor/volunteer appreciation events and other fundraising initiatives

Requirements:

- Must have a bachelor's degree in communications, marketing, business or related fields.

- Must have the preferred experience of 3-5 years within non-profit fundraising or outreach activities

- Must have outstanding written communication and presentation skills

- Must have strong experience preparing reports

- Must have a friendly, enthusiastic and positive attitude

- Must have a strong knowledge of social media and other basic marketing platforms

- Must be detail-orientated with the ability to manage multiple projects at a time

Volunteer Manager Duties and Responsibilities

The main goal of a volunteer manager is to ensure that an organization has enough volunteers to fulfill its service mission. To meet that goal, a volunteer manager must perform a variety of duties involving recruitment, training and program planning. I reviewed several volunteer manager job postings to determine the core duties associated with this job.

Recruit Volunteers

Recruiting volunteers is going to be crucial to your nonprofit ministry organization. I recruited 60+ volunteers at any given event of our nonprofit organizations. Volunteers can be a great asset because they are passionate about serving, and they are willing. Our goal is to have only 3% of our funds allocated toward our operation costs and the remaining allocated to fulfilling our mission.

When your organization is ready to recruit volunteers, you should use a variety of methods to attract qualified candidates. You may place advertisements in the newspaper, post volunteer opportunities online or attend job fairs with the hope of meeting new volunteers. Social media may also have potential volunteers in which you can see if they are a good fit for your organization.

Train Volunteers

Once a new volunteer comes on board, it's the volunteer manager's responsibility to provide comprehensive training. Volunteer managers often conduct orientation sessions, give new volunteers tours of your building, and help new volunteers get settled into their roles. In some cases, the volunteer manager also teaches volunteers new skills.

Create Program Reports

Without the right data, it's difficult to determine if a volunteer program is meeting its goals. Volunteer managers collect data from volunteers and paid staff members, use the data to create reports, and distribute those reports to key personnel in the organization.

Schedule Volunteers

The volunteer manager works closely with volunteers to come up with a schedule that works for everyone. If the organization has a special event planned, the volunteer manager is also responsible for ensuring that the right numbers of volunteers are available to handle the extra work.

Determine the Need for Volunteers

Some volunteers stay with the same organization for years, but others stop volunteering after just a few months. A volunteer manager must be able to anticipate these changes and plan accordingly.

Volunteer Manager Skills

This position involves a great deal of contact with other people, so a volunteer manager must have excellent interpersonal communication skills. A volunteer manager should also be able to use Microsoft Office programs to log volunteer hours, make volunteering schedules and create reports.

There must be a chief volunteer officer. As the chief volunteer officer, the board chair is responsible for leading the board. This position demands exceptional commitment to the organization, first-rate leadership qualities, and personal integrity. The chair must earn the respect of fellow board members to be able to meet the challenges of this position. Check out the Bible scripture of an example of a person of leadership qualities in 2 Timothy 2:23-26.

2 Timothy 2:23-24 (NIV)

"Don't have anything to do with foolish and stupid arguments, because you know they produce quarrels. And the Lord's servant must not be quarrelsome but must be kind to everyone, able to teach, not resentful."

Here is an Example of a Volunteer's Application Form

Thank you for your interest in serving at _____! We value our volunteers and know that so much of what we do for the youth that we serve would not be possible without the support of a caring community.

Below is a checklist to help ensure that you have completed all of the necessary documents needed to become a _____ volunteer. Once your package is complete, please bring the items indicated below and a $25 payment for the background check to our next orientation on February_____.

Volunteer Application Package Checklist Form (Example)

☐ Signed Volunteer Application

☐ Signed _____ Background Check Consent Form

☐ Signed GBI Criminal History Consent Form

☐ Payment for background check

    o Volunteers are asked to pay a fee of $25.00 for the background check.

    o Payment should be check or money order made out to

☐ Printed confirmation of Completion of Online Child Abuse Prevention Training

Abuse Prevention Training Form (Example)

_____ Volunteers are required to provide proof of completion of _____ abuse prevention training. To complete the training, **please read** over the following information and we will go over it in detail during the training.

Note: Please use pen when filling out the application. Print neatly and clearly.

Individual Volunteer Form		
Volunteer Information		
Name:		
Address:		
Phone:	Email:	
How did you learn about _____ ?		
☐☐Friend/Family ☐☐Hands On Atlanta		
☐☐Coworker ☐☐Volunteer Match ☐☐Other: _____		
☐☐Volunteer Event ☐☐ Website		
Have you ever worked or volunteered for _____ ?		
☐☐Yes ☐☐No	If Yes, Location: _____ Dates:_____ Title: _____	

What volunteer opportunity interests you?	
□□Youth Specialist Volunteer	□□Clothing & Toiletry Closets
□□Life Skills Volunteer □□In-kind Specialist Volunteer	□□Landscaping & Cleaning
□□Street Outreach Volunteer	□□Prepare & Share a Meal

Availability:			
Weekdays:	□Morning	□Afternoon	□Evening
Weekends:	□Morning	□Afternoon	□Evening

Emergency Contact Information
Name:
Address:

Phone:	Relationship to Volunteer:

Volunteer Signature

Signature:	Date:

Background Check Consent Form

We (_____) will obtain one or more consumer reports or investigative consumer reports (or both) about you for employment purposes. These purposes may include hiring, contracting, assignment, promotion, re-assignment, and termination. The reports will include information about your character, general reputation, personal characteristics, and mode of living.

We will obtain these reports through a consumer reporting agency. Our consumer reporting agency is General Information Services, Inc. It is based on the state in which you reside.

To prepare the reports, GIS may investigate your education, work history, professional licenses and credentials, references, address history, social security number validity, right to work, criminal record, lawsuits, driving record, credit history, and any other information with public or private information sources. The records search will go back through 7 years of residency.

You may inspect GIS's files about you (in person, by mail, or by phone) by providing identification to GIS. If you do, GIS will provide you help to understand the files, including trained personnel and an explanation of any codes. Another person may accompany you by providing identification. If GIS obtains any information by interview, you have the right to obtain a complete and accurate disclosure of the scope and nature of the investigation performed.

Please sign below to acknowledge your receipt of this disclosure.

_____   _____
Signature   Date

_____
Printed Name

GBI Authorization

Authorization: By signing below, you authorize: (a) General Information Services, Inc. ("GIS") to request information about you from any public or private information source; (b) anyone to provide information about you to GIS; (c) GIS to provide us (_____) one or more reports based on that information, and (d) us to share those reports with others for legitimate business purposes related to your employment.

The Federal Trade Commission provides a summary statement of your rights on its website at www.ftc.gov/credit. This summary is attached.

Personal Information:

Please print the information requested below to identify you for GIS.

Print name:	First	Middle	Last	Maiden

Other names used:	

Current and former addresses:

from Mo/Yr	to Mo/Yr	Street	City, State & Zip
from Mo/Yr	to Mo/Yr	Street	City, State & Zip
from Mo/Yr	to Mo/Yr	Street	City, State & Zip

Some government agencies and other information sources require the following information when checking for records. GIS will not use it for any other purposes.

Date of birth	Social security number
Driver's license number & state	Name as it appears on license
Signature	Date

Congratulations! You are almost ready to file for your 501©3 status. Your next step is to write your nonprofit ministry business plan.

Trust Him! - Listening Prayer

Hebrews 10:23-24 (MSG)

"Let's keep a firm grip on the promises that keep us going. He always keeps his word. Let's see how inventive we can be in encouraging love and helping out."

CHAPTER 11
WRITE THE NONPROFIT MINISTRY PLAN

What Should I do before I Write my Nonprofit Ministry Business Plan?

1. Research, Research, Research

2. Determine the purpose of your plan

3. Document all aspects of your business

4. Have a strategic marketing plan in place

5. Explain why you care

What Goes in the Body of Your Nonprofit Ministry Business Plan?

The Executive Summary

An executive summary of your business plan provides the reader with a snapshot of your company profile and goals.

Business Overview

A company overview (also known as company information or a company summary) is an essential part of a business plan. It's an overview of the most important points about your company—your history, management team, location, mission statement and legal structure.

Operations Plan

An operational plan can be defined as a plan prepared by a component of an organization that clearly defines actions it will take to support the strategic objectives and plans of upper management. Look at the operational overall planning process within the ministry organization.

Market Analysis

A business plan is the blueprint for taking an idea for a service and turning it into a reality.

a. Define your target consumers

    b. Explain what market you need to satisfy

c. Analyze the industry

    d. Identify market trends

    e. Provide a competitive analysis

    f. Draft a short summary of the market analysis

    g. Adjust the other sections of your business plan

Budget

A budget outlines your organization's financial and operational goals, so it may be thought of as an action plan that helps you allocate resources, evaluate performances, and formulate plans. A budget is an important part of your ministry business plan.

Habakkuk 2:2 (MSG)

"And then God answered, 'Write this. Write what you see. Write it out in big block letters so that it can be read on the run."

Congratulations! You wrote your nonprofit ministry business plan.

Are You Trustworthy? - Listening Prayer

1 Timothy 3:4-5 (MSG)

"He must handle his own affairs well, attentive to his own children and having their respect. For if someone is unable to handle his own affairs, how can he take care of God's church?"

CHAPTER 12
THE COST

How to Create a Nonprofit Ministry Business Budget:

1. Examine Your Revenue

2. Subtract Fixed Costs

3. Determine Variable Expenses

4. Set Aside a Contingency Fund for Unexpected Costs

5. Create Your Profit & Loss Statement

Conclusion

A nonprofit ministry business plan conclusion doesn't need to be very long. In fact, it can be pretty brief. Your conclusion should reiterate the opportunity, highlight the key strengths of your plan, summarize your vision, and remind the reader why your business is in a position to successfully execute the plan.

The conclusion basically asks us to do a few things:

1. Restate the main idea of the paper (why you wrote this entire long piece to begin with).

2. Summarize all the key points you made throughout the body of the paper (things that proved your thesis statement).

Budget Sheet Example

Monthly Cash flow Projection				
Enter Company name				
Enter Date Here				
	Pre-startup	Jan	Feb	Mar
1. Cash On Hand Beginning of month				
2. Cash Receipts				
(a) Cash Sales				
(b) Collections from Credit Accounts				
© Loan or Other Cash Injection				

Maintaining Your Budget

When maintaining a proper budget it gives your nonprofit ministry organization proper control. The budget paints a picture of how much cash is coming in and how much is going out. Budgets form the basis for boards to make better decisions and to avoid making mistakes. Budgeting allows boards to put limits on certain expenses as necessary and work to increase income sources early when it looks like there may be a shortfall. Monitoring the budget also provides an opportunity for board directors to move money around to allocate it efficiently as their cash flow changes.

Most importantly, nonprofit budgets should be constructed around the organization's programs and activities, which will help them stay focused on their goals.

Evaluating a Nonprofit Budget

The two primary components of a budget are income and revenue, and many subcategories fall under the umbrella of each.

It typically requires getting income from multiple sources for nonprofits to thrive. The budget lists all of those sources and provides an indication of the amounts the board can expect to come in from each source. Fundraising is a primary activity for nonprofit boards. Funds raised may come from ticket sales, membership fees, proceeds of auctions, galas, sales of goods or services, or other fundraising activities.

Under the heading of expenses, boards need to focus expenditures on their programs and activities. Expenses include direct costs, such as the cost of hiring new staff, ordering supplies, providing brochures or other publications, and ordering supplies and travel. Capital expenditures are expenses needed to acquire or maintain fixed assets, such as fixing or maintaining buildings, land and cars. Indirect costs, which are also called overhead, include things like utility bills, internet fees and postage.

It's important to be realistic in reviewing income sources and expenses. Board of directors should be careful to consider the state of the economy and any unusual or unforeseen financial situations of their contributors.

Grant-makers have the potential to contribute large sums to nonprofits and board directors should ensure that they meet the grantor's requirements to qualify. Donors expect to know how their donations are helping the organization, so boards need to consider how they can communicate this information to their donors.

It's rare that nonprofits have unlimited funds, so they need to be realistic and thoughtful about setting restrictions on what they can spend money on.

Developing the Nonprofit Budget

All board directors should have a good understanding of the purpose of the budget and their responsibility for developing a good working budget that supports the mission and that will lead the organization to sustainability. Your board should be your number one supporter with their own giving, and it should be at a 100% board giving.

Boards should begin reviewing their budgets at least three months before the end of the fiscal year. This is important so that the board will have time to approve the annual budget before the start of the next year. It helps to establish a timeline with a target date for board approval.

When you have your first budget planning meeting, the board or budget committee should agree on their financial goals. This will require prioritizing program delivery goals and setting organizational financial goals. This is a good time to review the current year's actual income and expenses against the budget. Boards should analyze variances and consider if there will be any impact on the upcoming budget. This is also a prime opportunity to clarify the annual goals from the strategic plan.

The second meeting of the budget committee should focus on developing a draft of an expense budget and an income budget. The committee will need to determine the costs for the upcoming program goals, organizational goals and strategic goals. In determining the income budget, the committee will need to project income based on the current fundraising and revenue activities.

At this point, the budget committee should have a draft budget ready and do a thorough review of it. The review should include verifying that the budget is able to meet program and organizational goals. Budget planning includes some degree of forecasting and assumptions and boards should thoroughly vet assumptions before finalizing the budget. They should make any final adjustments based on the organization's goals and its capacity to match income and expenses as closely as possible. In addition, they should review the final draft against the organization's goals and objectives.

Finally, the board or budget committee should be ready to present the annual budget to any necessary committees and the board for final approval.

Nonprofit budgets should be considered flexible documents. Many unexpected things can happen that greatly impact the budget. Revenue may not come in as expected, and large unexpected expenses can creep up. With proper budget planning, nonprofits can easily reap the benefits of good budgeting. Technology is an important tool for responsible budgeting for nonprofits.

The Benefits to Budgeting for Nonprofits

Good budgeting demonstrates accountability and transparency, which are important issues that donors and grant-makers look for before offering funds. Donors want to know where their money will be going. Good budgets assure donors that the nonprofit is actively overseeing the budget process. Having a good budget assists the board directors as well.

What Should be Included in an Operating Budget?

What is an operating budget for a non- profit? The annual **operating budget** is associated with the Statement of Activities (SOA), sometimes called the Income Statement or Profit & Loss, and involves projecting income and expenses for a single fiscal year to accomplish an organization's immediate mission agenda.

When you're planning an event, be sure to stay within your budget. To do that, you need a detailed event budget that you and your board agree on. Keeping an eye on an event budget will help you stay organized and prepared for any inquiry, all while keeping you from going over budget. Avoid going shopping without a budget, list or items needed. A good focus scripture I use and stand on is **Luke 14:28-30 (NIV)** "Suppose one of you wants to build a tower. Won't you first sit down and estimate the cost to see if you have enough money to complete it? For if you lay the foundation and are not able to finish it, everyone who sees it will ridicule you, saying, 'this person began to build and wasn't able to finish.'"

The annual budgeting process: a necessary exercise involving crunching numbers until you arrive at an estimated idea of how much money you will raise versus spend throughout the year, of course, which you hope your board will approve. For most organizations, developing a budget is a headache and the process that many leaders dread each year. However, considering the following strategies you can truly help the process, and make it easier, more efficient and more accurate.

Here are a few tips:

1) **Use a template** - I use QuickBooks for now; however, there are many good bookkeeping tools out there. You can begin with a general template that defines your main revenue sources and contains basic expense line items such as personnel costs. (Salaries, office expenses, rent, utilities, copying, supplies, travel, airfare, hotel, and meals). You can build out the line items in greater detail as you continue to develop your budget but starting with these will give you a good start.

2) **Minimize your line items** - Avoid adding too many line items. This can cause your budget to become overly complicated and lengthy.

3) **Budget weekly or monthly, whichever is easier for you** - Use a format that allows you to budget your activity per month of your fiscal year, rather than on an overall annual basis. This allows you to track your monthly progress accurately and foresee any realignment that may be needed earlier, so you can reallocate funds or plan to raise more revenue if needed. Focusing on shorter time periods helps break down the specific activities that will occur per month and account for special events, one-time costs, etc. **For example:** Every year, we have a Christmas Breakfast & Coat Drive for children in the community. We have put on this event every year, and every year the budget gets higher and higher. We budget and we plan a year in advance, by building partnerships throughout the year, and keeping our existing partners informed.

We make requests in advance for items such as: gift cards, coats, volunteers, supplies, and toys. We have never had an event where a child left without a new coat or toy.

4) Create an annual total - Include an overall annual column to roll each monthly to estimate up to the budget on a year-to-date basis. Having the overall view, along with the month-to-date view, will allow you to measure progress against the overall goal as you move through the fiscal year.

5) Account for inflation - Use prior year results as an estimate to begin from. Be sure to account for inflation (roughly 3 percent) for the following year. When creating a multi-year budget, account for inflation on each line item, over each year.

6) Consider you're fixed and necessary costs first - Start with the fixed costs you know you will have regardless of activity level and that you need to cover such as rent, utilities, salaries and insurance. Then, build in the variable costs. Have a list of the wants that you can add into your budget if you have projected funds left over after all the necessary expenses are covered.

7) Divide annual costs out by month - For line items that are easy to estimate on an annual basis and are relatively consistent, divide the annual amount by the number of months left in your fiscal year to arrive at your monthly amount.

8) Account for timing inconsistencies - Consider seasonality and timing of when revenue and expenses will come in and out, such as for events, annual appeal revenue drives, large gifts, etc. Make sure to understand the months that may have more revenue coming in or more expenses going out so you can plan to pay certain expenses when you have the cash or reserve enough cash to cover those expenses later.

9) Use prepopulated templates - Create tools such as general templates to help develop estimates for areas where revenue or expenses are consistent and repetitive such as travel or revenue proposals. **For example,** assign an average amount for gas ($100), business phone ($55), etc., to quickly calculate costs throughout the year.

10) **Calculate dependent line items from known costs** - Use known values to budget for other related estimates such as personnel costs. You can create a detailed personnel tab of your budget by listing each salary for the year and calculating bonuses, benefits/taxes, etc., as a percentage of the known salary. A standard rule of thumb is to include a 3 to 5 percent bonus and benefits/tax costs at a rate of 25 to 30 percent of each employee's salary.

When creating a nonprofit ministry budget, take time and lots of thought to develop. Remember to involve leadership from your nonprofit ministry organization to contribute the necessary details and accurate information to your budget. Maintain your bank account up to date.

Nonprofit Tax and Accounting Regulations

Two things to be aware of are GAAP and IRS requirements.

GAAP: The Generally Accepted Accounting Principles (GAAP) is guidelines that all accounting professionals must follow. They cover both for profit and nonprofit tax rules. It's imperative that accountants and financial professionals understand the current GAAP rules and any changes that happen throughout the years.

IRS Requirements: When filing and claiming your tax-exempt status, you definitely need to be aware of nonprofit IRS requirements.

Create a Multi-Year Plan that Supports Your Strategic Plan

Ask yourself where will your nonprofit ministry be in 3 years, 5 years? By creating a multi-year financial plan, you can support your nonprofit's growth. If you want to raise a certain amount of money by year 2025, you'll probably need to hire some employees, look at upgrading your fundraising/accounting software, and create some amazing marketing campaigns. By planning for it, you're able to support that growth and keep your board members encouraged and engaged.

Congratulations! You have completed your first annual budget.

May My Weakness be My Strength? - Listening Prayer

2 Corinthians 12:9 (MSG)

"And then he told me, 'My grace is enough; it's all you need. My strength comes into its own in your weakness.' Once I heard that, I was glad to let it happen. I quit focusing on the handicap and began appreciating the gift. It was a case of Christ's strength moving in on my weakness."

CHAPTER 13
S.W.O.T

W hat is SWOT? According to Liveplan.com - **SWOT** stands for strengths, weaknesses, opportunities, and threats. ... A **SWOT analysis** organizes your top strengths, weaknesses, opportunities, and threats into an organized list and is usually presented in a simple two-by-two grid. (Apr 5, 2018). Creating an S.W.O.T for your nonprofit ministry business plan is essential to understanding your need for your ministry non-profit organization.

Strength: (Experience)

Internal - How can my nonprofit ministry business capitalize on the strengths and become even stronger?

Example: As a nonprofit, we should be able to respond quickly to others in need.

Weaknesses: (Lack of Resources)

Internal - Analyze weaknesses to determine which can be negated or with some effort turned into a new strength for the organization.

Example: Need stronger accounting system, organization is not well known

Opportunities: (Conditions that benefit Your Organization)

External - Is your organization taking advantage of the opportunities that have been identified or are the opportunities slipping through the cracks and remaining lost revenue potential?

Example: Meeting New People/Building strategic relationships

Threat: (Negative economic, social)

External - Can you identify the threats of new opportunity, if viewed from a different perspective?

Example: Large organizations take time to gain relationships for grants

Strengths:

Staff	Sales Channels
Customer	Products/Services
Base	Profitable
Market Position	Growing

Weaknesses:

Staff Profit Margins to Love	Financial Resources
Competitive Vulnerability	Market Position

Lack of New Products	Lack of Services
Sales Channels	

Opportunities:

New Complimentary Market	Products
Strategic Alliance	Services
Funding	Position for Growth
Grants	Competition Weaknesses

Threat:

Economy	New Technology
Loss of Volunteers/Board Members	New Government Regulations
Lack of Financial Resources	Failing Grants
Cash Flow	Decreasing Funding

Now Complete Your Nonprofits Ministry SWOT:

Strengths –

Weaknesses-

Opportunities-

Threats-

Congratulations! You created your S.W.O.T for your ministry nonprofit organization plan.

A Community attracts the Holy Spirit - Listening Prayer

1 Peter 4:8-10 (MSG)

"Most of all, love each other as if your life depended on it. Love makes up for practically anything. Be quick to give a meal to the hungry, a bed to the homeless - cheerfully. Be generous with the different things God gave you, passing them around so all get in on it: if words, let it be God's words;"

CHAPTER 14

BRINGING AWARENESS

How I Planned my First Event to Raise Awareness and Funds?

According to charityhowto.org, a nonprofit ministry event budget is an important evaluation tool for goal setting. A nonprofit event has five goals – fundraising, raising awareness for the organization, raising awareness of an organization's programs, cultivation, and appreciation. The event's budget plays into the profitability portion of those goals (Sep 27, 2019).

One of the most common questions I have had to answer has been if nonprofits ministries are required to have a budget when planning a small event? Budgets are essential for nonprofits ministries in the success of achieving their goals and mission. From my experience, managing our nonprofit ministry cash flow efficiently has created a better financial sustainability.

Why Do I Need a Budget for my Event?

First and foremost, you want to have a realistic fundraising plan. When you're planning your fundraising strategy, it can be really easy to get wrapped up in the excitement and think that you'll be able to raise all the money in the world for your cause. Your passion to believe your cause is the best, right? Who wouldn't want to donate and support your mission?

However, we all know plans don't often go exactly as planned. The same can happen to your amazing, well put together fundraising strategy.

To prevent this, set realistic fundraising goals and plans. Use historical data to set your upcoming goals and develop a plan with these figures in mind.

If you're planning on using new tools or fundraising techniques, consider lowering your goal a bit until you feel comfortable that your new tactic will work.

And don't be afraid to change your plans or goals if you find that you won't be able to achieve them. There's nothing wrong with adjusting plans to reflect a new strategy.

A good budget can provide outside companies granting money or other resources to the organization a financial plan based upon accountability, transparency, and good faith. When planning a fundraiser event and to achieve a successful goal, it is extremely important to create a well-planned out budget. Building a budget is extremely important for nonprofit organizations to achieve a successful goal for their fundraiser events. I have found so many different tasks and check lists for our event budget, but here is one I have made some good use of from wildapricot.com.

Here is a list of tasks to consider for your event budget:

1. Track site rental

2. Estimate catering costs

3. Transportation charges

4. Entertainment and equipment fees

5. Summarize printing charges

6. Create a line item for gifts bags

7. Identify any activity expenses

8. Summarize projected expenses

9. Estimate expenses

10. Summarize actual expenses

For a basic event, such as a gala, Excel or other spreadsheet programs can be helpful. List the following four categories along the top: **item, projected expense, actual expense, details.** From there, you just fill in the spreadsheet and manage it like you would any other part of your business.

1. **Track site rental costs** - As you plan the event itself and as you meet with your board, track all projected rental fees for the event and function space, photographer, and other related expenses.

2. **Carefully estimate catering costs** - This includes all food and beverage charges and catering budgets. Managing them with care is a good idea, as they can be a great source of savings.

3. **Transportation charges** - This includes shuttles, event transfers and any related expenses. Don't forget insurance, fuel, tolls, or trailers if they are needed.

4. **Document entertainment and equipment fees** - Common expenses in this category include the A/V equipment, but it's also a good spot to list speakers or if you are hiring entertainers.

5. **Summarize printing charges** - Several small item charges actually combine to make a larger expense line item. These include invitations, name badges, program booklets, event signage, and banners.

6. **Create a line item for gift bag giveaways** - One of my pet peeves is to always thank your guess by giving them a gift. So, whatever gift or gifts you provide, track the cost for them separately; you'd be amazed at how much these items can cost.

7. **Identify** any **activities expenses** - If your event includes activities such as golfing, tennis, spa, rafting, biking, or other activities, you will want to note the cost of these fees separately. Consider summarizing the total cost in your spreadsheet and attaching a breakdown.

8. **Summarize projected expenses** - As you build your event program, you will have a good projection of the total expenses. This is the information that you will share with the board members to make sure they are aware of the event budget so that there aren't any surprises later on.

9. **Give yourself a contingency fund category** - Depending on the size or complexity of an event, you may want to give yourself as much as up to 20% of the event budget here. Despite the best planning, charges are going to exceed projected plans with expenses that you never considered. This will help keep you from going over budget every time.

10. **Summarize actual expenses** - This happens after the event has concluded. Subtotal the invoices into the above 10 categories and document the actual budget. If extremely favorable, identify savings in actual budget

vs. the projected budget, demonstrating the value you brought to the role.

Event Budget Example

Monthly Cash flow Projection				
Enter Company name				
Enter Date Here				
	Pre-startup	est	act	difference
3. Cash On Hand Beginning of month				
4. Table clothes				
(c) Event Space				
(d) Food				

Count the Cost!

Congratulations! You have completed your first event budget.

Ask! - Listening Prayer

Luke 11:9-10 (MSG)

"Here's what I'm saying: 'Ask and you'll get; seek and you'll find; knock and the door will open. Don't bargain with God. Be direct. Ask for what you need. This is not a cat-and-mouse, hide-and-seek game we're in."

CHAPTER 15
ASK & YOU SHALL RECEIVE!

O ur first event as a nonprofit ministry organization was a Christmas breakfast for families living in motels. Initially, it was just supposed to be a hot meal for families living in motels. In my search for the aged out foster care youth, I discovered how many families were living in motels, and it was shocking.

Only 6 months after filing my 501c3 forms I had already established MOUs with several nonprofit organizations and had acquired a few corporate sponsors by this time. I sent out a **Call to Action Letter** to all of my friends, partners, and sponsors asking for their assistance. My Call to Action was a success my partners and sponsors jump on board without any hesitation. One of my partners donated over 200 fully loaded gift bags, toiletries, stuff animals, and children's books.

We began our outreach to posted sign-up sheets in 15 motels. Being led by God, we then decided to collect brand new coats to give away as well. When I tell you coats came from everywhere, we collected over 216 brand new coats and 32 used ones. To top it off, someone heard what we were doing and dropped off a whole room full of toys. To this day, I don't know who she was, but we thank God for her.

One partner donated Nike sneakers. Another partner donated school supplies, and another donated food including milk, bread, and TV dinners, all of which families living in motels needed. We had 40+ volunteers and over 100 women and children in attendance from 15 motels in DeKalb County. Every attendee left our event with a brand new coat - even the parents. Can I tell you something? Out of all that happened that day, there was one thing that blessed me the most.

For the breakfast, one of my partners provided a pot of grits to serve our attending families. Around 12 pm, one of my board members walked up to me and asked if I had eaten anything. I said, "No, but I would have loved to have had some of those grits." To my surprise, she returned back with a bowl of grits.

I went to my partner and asked if she'd cooked more grits or perhaps had more than one pot. She replied, "No," and explained how she couldn't believe how many people the one pot had fed. One pot of grits fed over 100 people, and HE even saved some for me. You see, God will provide in abundance to His people.

If you heard nothing I said, here is one thing you need to remember: God will provide for His people. Ask!

How to Acquire Donations?

Here are some legal questions, which may come up while you are asking for donations. While researching, I found the following site helpful: https://fortune.com/2018/07/17/irs-nonprofit-donor-disclosures/.

Do Nonprofits Have to Disclose Donors?

The U.S. Treasury Department announced it will no longer require nonprofit organizations to disclose the names and addresses of donors giving $5,000 or more, arguing this change doesn't affect the information legally available to the public. The new guidelines affect all tax-exempt Section 501(c) (3), groups except those registered under 501(c)(3), Politico reports.

What Are Nonprofits Required to Disclose?

Nonprofits must submit their financial statements, which include the salaries of directors; officers and key employees to the IRS on Form 990. Both the IRS and the nonprofit are required to disclose the information they provide on Form 990 to the public.

Are 501c3 Records Public?

The IRS requires all U.S. tax-exempt nonprofits to make public their three most recent Form 990 or 990-PF annual returns (commonly called "990s") and all related supporting documents. They must also make public their Form 1023, which organizations file when they apply for tax-exempt status (IRS.gov).

Most nonprofits operate on a short budget, which means that pulling in new financial donations on a regular basis is an absolute must. However, attracting new donors and donations isn't simple—it requires dedicated work.

By keeping the mission in mind that the more money your nonprofit raises and receives in-kind-donations, the more lives you are able to change.

Despite good intentions, many nonprofits stay stuck in financial survival mode – short on time, money, and resources.

When Asking for Donation Can Be Hard

Sometimes, asking for money can make you feel as though you are begging. I hear this all the time and trust me I've been there. Building a nonprofit ministry, you may need to raise more money than you may have ever expected. That's why, in my *One on One Coaching*, I teach you how to raise *big dollars* to fully fund your programs and events. Then, you will be able to spend more time on your nonprofit ministry's mission and less time worrying about how to raise money. One of our success keys to raising awareness and funding for your nonprofit ministry is to deliver the right message to the right people at the right time. Everything you share about your nonprofit ministry will either attract donors or cause them to turn away.

You want to get right to the point with thanking them in advance. For example, "I'm writing to you to ask you to support me and my (cause/project/etc.) Just a small donation of ($amount) can help me (accomplish task/reach a goal/etc.) Your donation will go toward (describe exactly what the contribution will be used for)."

Having the confidence to *ask* for whatever your nonprofit ministry needs without feeling you're begging. Sharing your story and your *why* will deliver a message that will inspire and encourage your donors to give. Donor-based fundraising isn't begging for money. It's about not being too proud to *ask*.

There is so much information out there on how to ask. I found nonprofitsource.com, which gives valuable tips and information and has had great success.

Tips on How to Ask For Donations from a Company by Mail

1. Do your homework before sending donation request.

2. Learn their procedures and follow them.

3. Express your appreciation.

4. Share a brief summary of your mission.

5. Describe your nonprofits goals and what you'd like to achieve.

6. Let them know how to be supportive.

7. Send updates once the project or event is over.

How to Ask a Local Company for Donations?

Asking your local company in your community is one of the most successful ways to build your organization. When asking for donations from local companies, first you must build a relationship with the business owner or the manager of the company. **Let's take Wal-Mart for example**: How often do you visit. If often, do you know the name of the manager? I ask this for two reasons:

1. If you don't know the manager, he/she doesn't know you. Many companies are now going to online donations, in-kind-donations and grants. One of the reasons for this is because it is getting out of control with nonprofits asking and the stores are not being responsible in their giving.

2. When applying for donations or grants online, you will need to provide the name of the manager of your local company. They will often ask if the manager recommends your organization for the donation or grant. As nonprofit organizations, we must not only go with our hands out, but with

our hands UP. We must seek and ask God how we can be a blessing to our communities. Then trust Him to lead us to our dedicated donors.

Here are some examples of making an *Ask*:

1. Ask.

2. Think of any companies you may have. existing contact with.

3. Meet new people.

4. Identify the right person to fit your mission.

5. Think about In-Kind-Donations.

6. Say thank you.

What Should I Do First When Asking for Donations in Person?

1. Build a strong relationship before you ask.

2. Meet them where they are.

3. Practice your elevator pitch.

4. Share your story and your WHY.

5. Be genuine and direct.

6. Thank them for their time.

7. Ask is there anything you can do for them.

8. Include links to your online donation page and contact information.

9. Ask for a small Amount.

10. Tell them how it will make a difference.

How Do I Ask for Donations Online?

1. A call to action.

2. Ask for smaller donations.

3. Ask in the moment.

4. Ask donors to give online at events.

5. Create Social Media awareness.

How Do I Gain New Donors?

Education giving saw relatively slower growth (3.6 percent) compared to the ... Only 3-5% of Americans who give to their local church do so through regular tithing. ... 3 out of 4 people who don't go to church make donations to nonprofits ... People who volunteer report that they feel better emotionally, mentally and physically.

While the majority receives their donation dollars from average U.S. households, don't assume that a single, wealthy donor is the easiest way to access a steady flow of cash donations, that's not usually the case. Instead, it's really the average individual who provides the funds that supports nonprofits in order to survive. These individuals are all around you, but you may have missed them, because you didn't make *The Ask*. The best way to receive donations is to ask these simple questions:

- What relationships have you built?
- Know your potential donors?
- Does the person care about your mission?
- Will they share your mission with family and friends?
- Can you strengthen old relationships?

How Do I Find New Individual Donors?

1. Your board is the key. Ask them for assistance?

2. Ask old donors to increase their giving.

3. Build NEW relationships.

4. Update your organization's website with compassionate stories.

5. Expand your outreach.

6. Volunteer/partner up at other non-profit ministry events.

How to Attract Donors

How often are you showing up in the public? In order to pull in more donors, it's important to expose your nonprofit to the public. Host events; invite the public to tour your facility. Find out what companies can send volunteers to get involved. Always look for opportunities to spread the word regarding your ministry's overall goals and mission. Reach out to corporations, schools, and businesses in your community that might have a vested interest in your mission. Social media funding through Network for Good Inc. campaigns are also good resources.

Building Relationships

Building Relationships is very important to many nonprofits. Most might assume that donors will be happy with the knowledge that their donations are helping to support a good mission. However, every nonprofit ministry should put in a little extra effort to show their appreciation to their donors. I personally deliver gift bags to each of my donors, send thank you cards, and pictures from the event to show how their donation made a difference in the lives of others. In addition to sending out personal thank-you cards and donation receipts, we also give our donors options to get more involved with our organization. We invite them to volunteer, ask them for advice, and offer them a place on our advisory board, and share the impact their donation has made. These are just a few ways to keep them engaged, so it's vital you let your donors know that you appreciate them. They could turn into the possibility of becoming long-term donors. Volunteers can be one of your most valuable donors.

Old Navy Donation Program

Through Old Navy (YCP) YourCause Program, the company offers grants for Old Navy's employees who volunteer with nonprofit organizations. Each Old Navy associate can request, match, or grant volunteer hours per organization throughout the year. Looking in the proper place, you can find this with most companies.

How Do I Find Nonprofit Donors?

For the most part, when I first started looking for donors, I was told to take a look at similar nonprofit organization's annual reports, websites, and newsletters; then I compile a list of who is giving to them. I looked at nonprofit ministries, who were doing great work and had been around for years. I made a prospective list of all the donors. I shared the list with my board members and asked if they happened to know anyone on the lists; if possible, could they give me an introduction. This is also a good way to keep your board engaged.

How Do Nonprofit Organizations

ASK

For In-Kind-Donations?

I remember a story from one of my MOU's partners; she shared with me that her nonprofit organization operated off of 3% of their gross income. This blew me away, so I asked her how it was even possible, and this is what she told me, "Crystal 97% of what the organization brings in is from In-Kind-Donations." Wow is right, and this gave me a whole new perspective on how to **ASK**.

Support.globe.com has a few suggestions:

1. Make a list of the companies whose products you use/find contact information.

2. Write a sincere letter expressing how much you love the products.

3. Wait until the end of the letter to ask for In-Kind-Donations.

You also have a few companies who provide free software, equipment, and services to nonprofits.

1. Tech Soup offers free technology for nonprofits (https://snowballfundraising.com/fundraising-software/).

2. YouTube's Nonprofit Program - helps nonprofits connect with supporters, volunteers, and donors. For many causes, video is a new but essential format for storytelling. With one billion viewers on **YouTube** every month, nonprofits of all sizes can use **YouTube** videos to share their stories with a global audience.

3. Nonprofits can receive free hosting through Acorn Host – www.acornhost.com

4. Good360 offers free equipment for your nonprofit business with a membership fee.

There is one thing about me; I've never been afraid to ask. I remember my first *Ask* like it was yesterday. It was with the owner of a corporate business. We had just started our mentoring program for girls' ages 5 to 17 years old. Our girls met in the mornings on Saturdays. We understood that breakfast was the most important meal of the day. We asked our new partner if he could donate breakfast for 25 girls as an In-Kind-Donation. By the end of 2019, we had established a great relationship and partnership. This relationship and partnership works both ways. On any given weekend he can find my family and I sitting down eating at his restaurant.

His company became one of my biggest supporters and sponsors. He donated over $3,500 in funds and in-kind-donations. Every year, I asked my MOU's partners to donate time, funds, and in-kind-donations for my events. You must be willing to ask, seek, and knock on doors to receive the funds for your mission. The Bible says we have not because we ask not. (James 4-2 MSG)

Here Are a Few Ways to Finding Corporate Donors:

Sharing my story and my elevator pitch have been successful in finding corporate donors. I gave them my elevator pitch first – Do You Know 25,000 Youth will Age-Out of Foster Care with No Place to Call Home? My Name is Crystal R. Durham – CEO of Ninety Days of Love Crisis Center. We assist youth with becoming self-sufficient. I would love to sit down with you over coffee and share with you to see if you are able to assist us in our mission.

Here are a few tips

1. Co-Workers and Employees

2. Personal Connections and Relationships

3. Board Members and Volunteer Connections

4. Followers on Social Media

5. Neighbors

6. Suppliers/Vendors

As your nonprofit ministry grows to a place of success, you will be in a position to attract big donors. Here are some tips I found on Socialvelocity.net that was very instrumental to our nonprofit ministry, and I'm trusting it will assist you as well.

How Can I Attract Big Donors?

1. Identify prospects.

2. Educate and cultivate your prospects.

3. Ask for support.

4. Thank and recognize those who gave in the past.

5. Invite them to an event as a guest.

6. Ask them to volunteer.

How Do I Get Businesses in My Community to Donate to My Mission?

I remember my first corporate sponsor and how it only happened because I was willing to share my mission story. I was looking for a part time-job for the holidays, and during the interview, I shared how I couldn't work on the 2nd and 4th weekends.

I shared the details of my nonprofit organization and the mentorship program, whom we met with on those days. The store manager over heard me and immediately interrupted the interview. He was not only impressed with my qualifications; he was excited to partner up with Ninety Days of Love Crisis Center, Inc. Till this day they are one of our biggest corporate supporters and sponsors.

Establishing partnerships and relationships with businesses in our community have been so instrumental in helping us fulfill our mission. I have found that most non-profit ministries aren't concerned with going after businesses in their communities. To be honest, they may not know how to pursue them. In talking with many, I have often recognized it is due to a lack of confidence and vision, or not knowing what to say.

In partnering up with businesses in our community, we have been able to achieve one of our main goals for the mission; bringing awareness. Without having a Mission *Ask* strategy, many times you may leave money on the table. Failing to have a mission, *Ask* strategy, or plan for your nonprofit ministry can and will cost the organization to struggle. Successful nonprofit ministries, such as The Red Cross, already have a mission, *Ask* strategy, and are reaping the financial benefits from it. Many companies often have money set aside for charitable causes. They often can donate or may be able to provide hands-on volunteer assistance, which can turn into grant money for the organization. Ninety Days of Love Crisis Center, Inc. has reaped this benefit from companies over and over. When asking local businesses and large companies, keep in mind they are used to getting solicitations from nonprofit ministries. This can make the donation process competitive, but it's one thing we have never feared.

Why? Our nonprofit ministry has created opportunities to stand out, and we also develop partnerships and relationships. This is why it's important to find ways to make your nonprofit ministry friendly and stand out. This is where your MOU's partnership can come in handy, creating partnerships with other nonprofit ministry organizations, who are also serving in your community. Making sure you and your board members have a good understanding of your ministry's needs and knowing how to approach a Business on your mission are vital for securing donations.

For example, when we have our annual Christmas breakfast and coat drive and we are looking for donations, we first ask our local businesses, whom we had already established relationships and partnerships with. Many of our partners have employees who were parents and they might know individuals or families with children in need of coats. Therefore, they already have an idea of who's going to benefit from their donations. Thus, they may be more willing to contribute.

For instance, we've had business managers donate gift cards. This strategy will bring people back into their stores later on. Sometimes, they may provide actual merchandise or gift bags. Often your nonprofit ministry can use these items for raffles. Making mention of these gifts that are associated with the business are goodwill promotional gestures that can help put companies in a positive light in the community.

I Have a Covenant with You! - Listening Prayer

Genesis 31:44-49 (MSG)

"So let's settle things between us, make a covenant - God will be the witness between us."

CHAPTER 16
A COVENANT PARTNERSHIP

These are all great ways to help fully fund your nonprofit ministry organization, but they're not the only ways. As I mention in the past chapter, one of the best impacted discussions I made with our nonprofit ministry organization was to develop MOU's (Memorandum of Understanding) Partnerships. Rocketlawyer.com has some of the best and informed information on what and how on **MOU's Memorandum of Understanding**. Here is what I found to help our nonprofit ministry.

What Is a MOU (Memorandum of Understanding)? A memorandum of understanding, MOU, is an agreement between two or more parties, outlined in a formal document. It is not legally binding but signals the willingness of the parties to move forward with a contract.

Why Do I Need a Memorandum of Understanding?

Generally, each party starts in a planning stage to determine what they want or need the other party to provide, what they have to offer, what they are willing to negotiate, and the rationale for an MOU. Perhaps most important, the MOU spells out the parties' common objectives.

What are the Differences Between a Contract and a Memorandum of Understanding?

A contract is a legally enforceable agreement between two or more parties that creates an obligation to do (or not do) a particular thing. Similar to a contract, a memorandum of understanding is an agreement between two or more parties. However, unlike a contract, an MOU does not need to contain legally enforceable promises.

Who Signs a MOU (Memorandum of Understanding?)

Signatures: A representative from each partner with authority to bind their organizations contractually should sign the MOU. Each partner should retain a copy of the signed agreement.

How Do I Write a Memorandum?

Steps

1. Type "MEMORANDUM" at the top of the page. State that this document is a memorandum at the outset.

2. Address the recipient appropriately.

3. Add additional recipients in the CC line.

4. Add your name to the *From* line.

5. Include the date.

6. Choose a specific phrase for the subject line.

7. Format the heading properly.

When Should a Memorandum of Understanding Be Used?

Companies often choose to use an MOU instead of a contract because it is a friendlier, bipartisan expression of a working relationship than a formal contract. MOUs are often used in cases where parties either do not want to imply a legal commitment or cannot create a legally enforceable agreement.

MOU (MEMORANDUM OF UNDERSTANDING) CONTRACT FORM EXAMPLE

MEMORANDUM OF UNDERSTANDING

BETWEEN

_____

AND

_____OF _____COUNTY

FOR COOPERATION RELATING TO STANDARDIZATION, CONFORMITY ASSESSMENT

_____

AND

_____OF _____COUNTY

Desiring to promote mutual interest through cooperation in the field of standardization, conformity assessment and legal metrology on the basis of equality and mutual benefit; Recognizing that such cooperation shall promote economic cooperation and support the friendly relationships between two agencies; and

Pursuant to the relevant provisions of the agreement relating to scientific and technical cooperation Between the
_____and
_____, signed on _____ hereinafter referred to as "the Agreement";

Have Agreed as Follows:

Article 1

The parties will support cooperation in the fields of (**providing** direction, guidance and technical **support** in the development of the original) standardization, conformity assessment and legal metrology – the practice and the process of applying regulatory on the basis of equality and mutual benefits, in accordance with the provisions of this Memorandum of Understanding (MOU), the agreement and the respective laws and regulation of the two businesses.

Article 2

Cooperation may include the following:

a. Joint or cooperative programs and projects of mutual benefit, including visits and exchange of children safety and other experts or educational information

b. Mutual cooperation in international and regional organizations relating to standardization, conformity assessment and legal metrology

c. Organizations of and participation in conferences, shelter, safety, health courses, workshops, exhibitions and other joint meetings of mutual interest

d. Exchange of technical data and information relating to standardization, conformity assessment and legal metrology

e. Operation of joint training/education programs to raise competency in standardization, conformity assessment and legal metrology

f. Other forms of co-operation as agreed by the parties, including meetings between the two parties on a regular basis.

Article 3

1. Cooperative activities under this MOU shall be subject to the availability of funds and personnel. The terms of financing shall be agreed upon in writing by the parties before the commencement of activities.

2. Whenever more than the exchange of information or exchange visits of individuals or promotion activities is planned to take place, such activity shall be described in a Project Annex to this MOU which shall set forth as appropriate to the activity, a work plan, staffing requirements, cost estimates, funding sources, and other undertakings, obligations, or conditions not included in this MOU.

Article 4

The parties should consult with each other before any information derives from cooperation activities under this MOU is disclosed for commercial purposes.

Article 5

1. Any issues arising from the interpretation or implementation of this MOU will be settled through consultations between the parties or such other means as they may mutually decide. The parties do not anticipate the creation of or exchange of intellectual property during the course of this MOU.

2. Notwithstanding paragraph 1 of this article, issues for the protection and distribution of intellectual property created or furnished in the course of cooperative activities under this MOU shall be settled in accordance with the provisions of Annex I of the agreement and the security obligations shall be settled in accordance with the provisions of Annex II of the agreement.

Article 6

1. This MOU shall enter in force upon signature by both Parties and remains in force for a period of one **(2) years, unless terminated earlier by either Party upon ninety (90) days, written notice to the other Party.**

2. The termination of this MOU shall not affect the validity or duration of projects under this MOU that are initiated prior to such termination.

IN WITNESS WHEREOF, the unsigned being duly authorized by the respective agencies, has signed this MOU.

Done on the _____of_____, _____, in the English.

FOR THE AGENCY_____

FOR THE AGENCY_____

Congratulations! You have established your first MOU's partnerships.

There are several different forms of agreement; another form of agreement is a Letter of Intent.

What is the Difference between a Letter of Intent and a (MOU) Memorandum of Understanding?

Investopedia.com states that a **Letter of Intent** is a document, often used in mergers and acquisitions, which records the preliminary terms of an agreement. The primary difference between the two is that a letter of intent is not binding, whereas a memorandum of understanding is considered binding and carries weight in a court of law.

What is the Purpose of a Letter of Intent?

The main purpose of a letter of intent (sometimes also referred to as a "Letter of Understanding" or "Memorandum of Understanding") is to facilitate the start of a business deal or project between the parties involved by identifying the key business and contractual understandings that will form the basis of the final.

How to Write a Letter of Understanding

1. Reference any previous meetings or correspondence.

2. Outline the terms discussed and the positions of both parties, making it clear what you agree on and what may need further discussion.

3. If your agreement requires a formal contract, remind the recipient of such.

Now that you have all the information, you will need to get started on building a successful nonprofit ministry. You need to know how to maintain and organize your nonprofit ministry, how and where to file all of your important documents. All important documents are filed in your corporate book. What's a Corporate Book? I'm glad you asked.

Keeping Order - Listening Prayer

1 Corinthians 14:40 (ESV) "But all things should be done decently and in order."

CHAPTER 17
MY CORPORATE BOOK

P utting all records in order is going to be vital to the growth of your nonprofit ministry organization. Allbusiness.com and Corpocationentre.ca helps you to do just that.

These records are typically kept in what is called a *Minute Book*. A corporate minute book holds all your important corporate documents; such as articles of incorporation, shareholder and director meeting minutes, tax filings, share certificates, by-laws and other legal documents, in one convenient registry. Maintaining corporate compliance is an essential function that begins with being organized. Ultimately, it's a job that starts with you, your company's owner, or secretary—and it doesn't have to be difficult or complicated.

How to Organize My Corporate Book

Your company corporate book is where you keep all your company's important paperwork, such as your state filing documents and company meeting minutes. As you update certain documents, such as the member ledger for your Inc., you will want to make sure to place the updated copies in your corporate book to keep it current. You will also want to keep your minute book handy for inspection at all times (for sponsor, donors, members, or even the IRS or state taxation agencies).

Examples of documents to include:

- **Articles of incorporation**

- **Corporate bylaws**

- **Operating agreement (Success Plan)**

If you are organizing a corporation book, start out by making sure that you have your original articles of incorporation from your state of formation. You will also need the corporate bylaws that you adopted during the setting up of your nonprofit.

Here is a list of other documents that should be in your corporate book:

- Meeting minutes and notices of meetings sent to members

- Documentation of adopting an operating agreement

- Documentation of adopting corporate bylaws

- Documentation of appointing a board of directors

- Documentation of bank accounts opened

- Documentation of approved contracts, grants received or requested

- Documentation of the authorization or rescinding the authority of an employee/volunteer to perform some function for the organization

- Documentation of the purchase, sale, or In-Kind-Donations of major assets

- Documentation of tax election

- Documentation of the approval of an independent audit of the company's financials

- Documentation of amending the articles of organization or corporate bylaws

- Documentation of employees hired or independent contractors

- Documentation of a corporate officer salary

- Documentation of the approval of a business transaction between the company and an individual owner or officer

- Documentation of the approval of a transaction that causes a conflict of interest

- Documentation of adopting employee benefit plans

- Documentation of adopting a corporate retirement plan

- Documentation of the details and when an insurance policy was established

- Documentation of approving a commercial lease

- Documentation of authorizing corporate credit cards for employees

- Documentation of authorizing expense accounts for employees

Basically, any major decision involving money, power or both should be recorded and filed in your corporate book. When in doubt, draw up a resolution and file it. It is better to have too much information in there than not enough.

You may assemble together certain business documents in your corporate book such as:

1. Assemble together:

- Journals that detail the organization's business transactions and affected accounts

- Ledgers for the fiscal year being audited

- Bank statement and canceled checks

- Payroll records and tax returns showing withholdings for employees

- IRS Form 1099's for independent contractors and consultants

- Tax returns (990, 990-T)

- Invoices and paid bills (Receipts)

2. Have organized and readily available all:

- Corporation or organizational documents

- Policies related to financial management and control

- Tax exemption letters

- Board or committee meeting minutes

- Grant proposals, commitment letters and contracts with funding sources

- Final reports submitted to funders

- Contracts with vendors

- Leases

- Equipment maintenance agreements

- Insurance policies (office contents, professional liability, etc.)

3. Reconcile All Bank Accounts

4. Prepare:

- Trail Balance (a report at the end of the accounting period that ensures debits equal credits

- Accounts receivable schedule

- Accounts payable schedule

- Depreciation schedules

- Expense account analyses requested by your auditor

- Schedules of prepaid expenses for the upcoming fiscal year

- List of fixed asset additions and dispositions

- Investment activities

Congratulations! Organizing your first corporate book.

I'm so proud of you and all that God has called you to do in your community. As I have said many times before, if He has called you to it, He will provide. Now that you have all the tools, information, and encouragement to **Build a Profitable Nonprofit Ministry**, you don't have to do it alone. My One on One Coaching for individuals such as yourself is on my website www.crystaldurham.com. If you need further assistants and someone to walk alongside of you, let's make a difference together.

Made in United States
Orlando, FL
07 November 2023

38687320R00085